Dunoon and the Cowal peninsula is an area that is emerging from the shadows. Promoted by its Tourist Board as "Scotland's best kept secret", this part of mainland Scotland has come to be regarded as an island, often by-passed by visitors en route to the Highlands, and considered "remote" by modern-day economic developers.

Yet with the demise of the U.S. Navy submarine base at the Holy Loch, for three decades a key economic landmark, the people of Dunoon and Cowal are facing the prospect of bringing their area into a changed world.

In this timely guide, Julian Hill, with contributions from several local people, charts the history, describes the archaeology, outlines the main features of a rich environment and extensive wildlife, and gives an invaluable account of modern day human activity.

DUNOON & COWAL - a guide, charting a beautiful part of Scotland that lies barely one hour by road from Glasgow city centre, is an essential point of reference for visitor and native alike.

DUNOON
&COWAL

a guide

Julian Hill

with contributions from
George MacLennan
Mairi Paterson
and Nigel Scriven

illustrations by Marcia Clark

Argyll
publishing

©Copyright Argyll Publishing 1992

First published in 1992 by
Argyll Publishing
Glendaruel
Argyll PA22 3AE

©Back cover map Bartholomew, Edinburgh

The right of Julian Hill to be identified as the author of this
work has been asserted by him in accordance with the
Copyright, Designs & Patents Act 1988.

British Library Cataloguing-in-Publication Data.
A catalogue record for this book is available from the
British Library.

ISBN 1 874640 00 9

Typeset by Bill McLean, Dunoon
Linotronic output by Cordfall, Glasgow
Printed by E & R Inglis, Dunoon.

This book has been published with the support of the following subscribers:

Argyll Mini Coach Tours Dunoon 0369 2293

Argyll Office Equipment Ltd. Argyll St Dunoon 0369 5276

Bookpoint Argyll Street Dunoon & Greenock 0369 2377

Chalmers W & J Estate Agents, Dunoon 0369 4097

Chatters Brasserie 58 John Street, Dunoon 0369 6402

County Garage, Dunoon 0369 3149

Clyde Property, 68 Drymen Road, Bearsden 041 943 0777

Creggans Inn Strachur 0369 86 279

Curiosity Shoppe Argyll Street, Dunoon 0369 2600

Drimsynie Leisure Centre Lochgoilhead 03013 247

Dunoon Community Centre, Edward Street 0369 4669

Eco Grain & Health Store Hillfoot Street, Dunoon 0369 5106

Esplanade Hotel West Bay Dunoon 0369 4070

Forestry Commission Forest Enterprise, Cowal Forest District 0369 84 666

Gateway Leisure Queen's Hall, Dunoon 0369 2800

Glendaruel Caravan Park & Sutlery 0369 82 267

Glendaruel Hotel Clachan of Glendaruel 0369 82 274

Hafton Holiday Lodges Dunoon 0369 6205

Hearth 'n Home Argyll Street, Dunoon 0369 4092

Holy Loch Farm Park Dalinlongart 0369 6429

Inglis E & R Printers & Publishers, Dunoon 0369 3218

Kames Hotel Tighnabruaich 0700 811489

Kilmun House Hotel Kilmun 0369 84 418

Kirn Variety Store Pier Buildings Kirn

LeisureVenture Ormidale House, Glendaruel 0369 82 266

One Fifty Newsagents 150 Argyll Street Dunoon 0369

Queen's Hotel Kirn 0369 4224

Strachur Centre Strachur 0369 86 221

Strone House Strone 0369 84 355

Susy's Tearoom Tighnabruaich 0700 811452

Tighnabruaich Sailing School 0700 811396

Workers' Educational Association West of Scotland District Glasgow 041 332 0176

Younger Botanic Garden Benmore 0369 6261

About the author:

Julian Hill...
is a Lancastrian who has lived in Cowal for the last
sixteen years. He is tutor-organiser in adult education
for the Workers' Educational Association; teaches his
geology specialism to groups and summer schools and
arranges other courses throughout Argyll & Bute on the
environment, local history and Gaelic.

and the other contributors...

Marcia Clark...
lives in Strachur, studied Fine Art in Newcastle, and has
an active interest in wildlife and conservation.

George MacLennan...
was born in Angus, but has lived in Cowal for twelve
years. He is a linguist and a teacher and writer in
Gaelic.

Mairi Paterson...
was born in Stirling, but her ancestors are all from
Argyll. She taught English in Dunoon Grammar School
and became President of Cowal Archaeological Society
and a member for eight years of the Ancient
Monuments Board for Scotland.

Nigel Scriven...
set up the Cowal Natural History Society; has a special
interest in ornithology and works at the Ardentinny
Outdoor Centre.

Foreword

This book is published at a time of great change and challenge in this area. It is full of fascinating and little known information and is compiled by local experts with real feeling for this beautiful and relatively unknown part of Scotland. I have lived here for over thirty years and, as the owner of a local hotel have a keen interest in promoting tourism in Cowal. This book is a welcome addition to the library of any prospective visitor.

Fitzroy Maclean of Dunconnel.

Fitzroy Maclean
Strachur House,
Strachur, Argyll.

June, 1992

Contents

Introduction

Visitors to Cowal arrive either by ferry from Gourock or by road from Glasgow and Loch Lomond. Either way Cowal's natural features are most appealing. The sea crossing from Renfrewshire reveals the Dunoon shore backed by forested hills and glens, with views of distant mountains. Spectacular penetrating sea lochs continue the wide vista of the Firth of Clyde. At any time of year such views are quite unforgettable, a perfect combination of sea, sky and land.

The landward approach is equally impressive. From the head of Loch Long the towering heights of the Arrochar Alps lend grandeur to Cowal. The road twists and turns through deep clefts in the uplands; precipitous slopes both hide then reveal panoramic views of an overwhelmingly glaciated landscape. Glen after glen is followed until, by the Kinglas Water, the route turns south into the peninsula bounded by two of Scotland's longest lochs - Fyne and Long.

Travelling into Cowal visitors are struck by the peace and tranquility of the landscapes of the Argyll Forest

Park. Three routes provide superb sea vistas - from St Catherines to Strachur the broad expanse of Loch Fyne is reminiscent of Norwegian fjords. Continuing beyond Strathlachlan along one of Cowal's quietest roads the sea views persist as far as Otter Ferry with its gigantic shingle spit. The second route combines rugged ground with deeply penetrating lochs -from Ardlamont to Colintraive - with some of the finest views above the Kyles of Bute, surely some of Europe's most dramatic scenery. The third route follows Loch Striven and the Firth of Clyde to Loch Long - from Inverchaolain to Ardentinny with Dunoon half way. This is the most populated route, but has superb sea vistas up, down and across the Clyde and its tributary lochs.

Three more routes cross the interior of Cowal. From Dunoon the main Glasgow road leaves the populated shores of Holy Loch to follow the deep cleft of Loch Eck, past Ben More to Strachur. From Dalinlongart the second route crosses west through lonely Glen Lean to Tarsan Dam, Loch Striven and Loch Riddon. From here the choice is to follow Glendaruel north to Loch Fyne through Cowal's biggest valley or turn west at Ballochandrain over a dramatic route to Otter Ferry which has stunning views (and sunsets) over Loch Fyne to the mountains of Jura, Scarba and Mull.

Finally many of Cowal's glens are easily explored by car or on foot - the routes into Lochgoilhead are Hell's Glen and Glen Mor. Both twist and turn to reach the head of the loch with its views down to the grim keep of Carrick Castle. Glen Finart and Glen Massan are two more glens which have outstanding natural features which enable the walker to explore the higher and more remote parts of Cowal.

Cowal's natural beauty provides a rich variety of wild habitats - from extensive forests, rough moorlands, remote glens to fast-flowing burns, broad straths, lochs, lochans and sandy bays. Such a profusion of natural habitats is reflected in the broad range of animal and bird species which thrive in Cowal - Red Deer, Otter, Wildcat, Fox and Hare are joined by over 100 species of birds breeding in the area.

Despite today's scattered rural population Cowal has a long history of human settlement. The complex origins of settlement are reflected in local placenames. Both Gaelic and Norse are present. The earliest folk have left important archaeological evidence of their lives - successive waves of Neolithic, Bronze and Iron Age peoples. Cowal boasts an impressive array of ruined castles from the turbulent "clan" period, while the spread of Christianity has left a more impressive series of religious foundations.

Dunoon and Cowal were transformed in the nineteenth century by tourism, with the opening of rail and steamer links from Glasgow to the Clyde. The age of the seaside villa had arrived. It was fashionable to go "doon the watter", to sail to Tighnabruaich and the Kyles. Dunoon expanded from a tiny clachan to a major Clyde resort and a Burgh within a few decades. Eventually that image changed and faded with the coming of mass car travel, alternative holidays and more discerning tourists. Masking the change was the arrival of the American Navy Base at the Holy Loch which was to dominate the area from the sixties to the early nineties.

Today Dunoon and Cowal face a more uncertain future which cannot rely on thousands of day trippers or thousands of American sailors. But Dunoon and Cowal are blessed with an outstanding natural inheritance and strong historical and cultural traditions which will guarantee its future in a world which increasingly values those attributes.

Scenery

The Cowal Peninsula, with its magnificent scenery of uplands, glens and lochs, is part of the Grampian Highlands, but it also lies close to the Central Lowlands of Scotland. The highest ground is in North Cowal around Ben Ime (1,011 m), Ben Arthur (the Cobbler 881 m) and Ben Donich (842 m), these peaks proving some of the best climbs in the district. Moving south through Cowal, upland becomes lower in altitude, though equally as craggy and dramatic, especially around Loch Eck (Beinn Mhor 741 m), Loch Striven (Cruach nan Capull 612 m) and the Kyles of Bute (Beinn Bhreac 454 m). The highest ground near Dunoon is the plateau at Bishop's Seat (505 m).

Deeply cut into the hard rock of the uplands are beautiful glens, scoured by massive ice sheets and glaciers in the recent geological past. Some glens were subsequently drowned by rising sea levels - such as Lochs Striven, Eck and Goil, but the deepest of all is Loch Fyne. Other Cowal glens display their glacial origins as fine "U"-shaped valleys such as Glen Croe, Glendaruel, Glen Lean and Glen Massan. So thorough was Ice Age erosion that Cowal's uplands were carved

Loch Eck

into blocks separated by deep glens. Glen Massan, for
example, leads south into Glen Tarsan and Glen Lean
and north via Garrachra Glen into Glen Shellish and
eventually Loch Eck.

Cowal scenery is most impressive where the hills drop
steeply into the superb fjord coastline. The sea lochs
surrounding the peninsula include the deepest Loch
Fyne, which attains depths in excess of 200 m off

Portavadie in West Cowal. The loch was eroded by ice along a fault-shattered belt between Cowal and Kintyre, merging with similar depths of water in the broad Sound of Bute. The Firth of Clyde, off Dunoon, attains l00 m in places and is eroded, like Loch Fyne, along faults, such as the Highland Boundary Fault. Both Loch Long and Loch Striven have depths of 80 m or more, but their tributary lochs - such as Holy Loch and the Kyles are much shallower. Similarly, Loch Eck, though a freshwater body now, was joined to the Clyde at the end of the Ice Age by higher sea levels. Today Loch Eck is shallow, barely 30 m deep in places.

The uplands of Cowal are built of hard, weather-resistant rocks, such as schists and quartzites, outcropping as craggy, knobbly features. Even tough rock, however, is broken down by weathering and erosion processes such as rain, frost and wind. Ice Age erosion had the most profound effects - huge glaciers bulldozed their way through Cowal, cutting deep valleys, breaking down rocks by freeze-thaw and ripping out bedrocks. All this occurred in very recent times, but even before that Cowal had suffered intense, prolonged weathering lasting tens of millions of years which provided the broad outline of uplands and valleys. The oldest features are perhaps ten million years old, the events of the Ice Age having greatly modified that ancient landscape.

A factor which facilitated Ice Age erosion was the arched-up arrangement of Cowal's rocks, a feature which is noticeable around the Loch Riddon-Loch Striven area. Here the bedrocks are folded into a large arch - the Cowal Arch - the edges of which point skywards. During the Ice Age, freeze-thaw processes cut deeply into the broken edges of the rocks and deep glens were carved at the critical keystone point in the arch. Thus, hard resistant rocks were carved up into an intricate maze of glens, corries, valleys and lochs. The direction of the largest valleys and lochs gives the clue to understanding the process - in Cowal these valleys run northwest to southeast at right angles to the strike of the arch - which is northwest to southwest.

The Rocks of Cowal

All rocks can be classified as sedimentary, metamorphic and igneous, according to their origins. Cowal has representatives of all three.

Sedimentary rocks form from compression of loose sediment laid down in seas or rivers, a good local example being Old Red Sandstone found around Toward, a former river sand derived from the breakdown of older rocks.

Metamorphic rocks are well seen in Cowal, They are hard rocks which formed from heat and pressure applied to older rocks deep in the Earth's crust.

Igneous rocks form from hot, liquid magma (melted rock) injected into the Earth's crust from below. Good local examples are the many "dykes" in Cowal. One of the largest forms Castle Hill, Dunoon. Cowal does not possess any lava flows (the nearest form the hills of Renfrewshire) or granite (the nearest occurs in Glen Fyne).

From the geological map it is easy to follow the main rock types in Cowal. The main division is the Highland Boundary Fault which cuts across South Cowal from Innellan to Toward Castle. The fault separates metamorphic schists, slates and quartzites from Old Red Sandstone and Midland Valley rocks.
The main mass of rock in Cowal is Dalradian Metamorphic - belts of essentially foliated or slatey rocks striking northeast to southwest. Many are schists and quartz rocks forming the highest ground in Cowal from Ben Ime to Beinn Mhor. Dunoon gives its name to the Dunoon Phyllites, slate-like rocks pale grey/green in

colour and well exposed along Dunoon's East Bay, Kirn and Hunter's Quay shores. At Bullwood a sandy schist is quarried for building stone and the Kirn area once had quarries in phyllite.

The commonest minerals seen around Dunoon are quartz - a white crystalline rock and mica - a sparkling mineral found in the phyllites and schists. Further north the minerals along Loch Eck change to brown mica (biotite) and at Strachur brown/red garnets are common in the schist. The changing minerals reflect greater heat and pressure applied to the rocks when they were buried ten miles down in the Earth's crust.

In West Cowal the rocks are more varied than the schists further east. Around Tighnabruaich the quartz-mica schists of the Cowal Arch form high ground. In Glendaruel the schists change to the "green beds", some of the most unusual rocks in the area because they represent beds of volcanic ash dating from a time when volcanoes erupted in West Argyll and their ash blew east to fall into seawater which then lay over Cowal. West Cowal also has a limestone outcrop, seen at Kilfinan and Otter Ferry where it was once burnt for agricultural lime.

In South Cowal the geology changes abruptly from schists to Old Red Sandstone along the line of the Highland Boundary Fault.   South of Innellan Pier are beds of brown sandstone and pale limestone (cornstone) which run all the way to Toward Point and west to Toward Castle, where the Highland Boundary Fault brings in the schists again. Along this shore are good exposures of black-weathered dykes, sheets of once-molten rock forced up into cracks in the sandstone. Many of the dykes had their origins far from

Cowal, in the bowels of recently-active volcanoes in Mull and Arran.

Dunoon's most prominent landform - Castle Hill - has a surprisingly interesting geological history. The hill is built from a thick dyke dating back 300 million years which was injected nearly vertically into phyllite as a molten mass. The dyke can be traced west as far as Jura and east to Edinburgh.

None of Cowal's rocks contain fossils. The schists and igneous rocks by their very nature and origins could not have had organisms present which could have survived as fossils. However, recent research has found possible algal fossils in some of the Dunoon Phyllites as a rare survival. Old Red Sandstone was a river deposit and no life forms survived that process intact. Ironically it is the Ice Age which has left the most fossil evidence in the form of glacial shells preserved in the muds of higher sea levels 12,000 years ago in the Kyles of Bute.

Geological History

The oldest rocks are the Dalradian metamorphics forming some 600 million years ago as ocean floor mud and sand. In those times (Pre-Cambrian) British geography was very different from now - Scotland was part of a large slab of Earth's crust (a plate) which included Greenland and North America long before the Atlantic Ocean formed. England was on a different plate with much of Europe. Both plates were 30° **south** of the Equator in what is now Southern Africa. The ocean sediment formed in great thicknesses (several miles thick) swept along by undersea currents into deep troughs. Volcanic activity pierced the ocean floor in West Argyll (the origin of the green beds of Glendaruel), lime muds formed on shallower banks in the sea and Dunoon's Phyllites are thought to have accumulated in quite shallow, almost estuarine, conditions.

About 500 million years ago the ocean closed, bringing the plates together along a northeast-southwest collision zone. The crustal collision was of gigantic proportions affecting many continents producing a dramatic change in Scottish geography. A lofty mountain chain developed (the Caledonian Mountains) from the great pile of ocean sediment right across Scotland, with mountains of Alpine-Himalayan proportions. Since then the Caledonian Mountains have undergone almost continual erosion, thus reducing them to their roots - it is these roots which form Cowal's hills today.

Ironically the rocks of Cowal are upside-down from their original seafloor position. The plate collision produced huge folds of rock, turning the Dalradian sequence right over in an enormous over-fold - or nappe - which stretches from Kintyre to Perthshire. The crest of the fold is the Cowal Arch and results in steeply inclined rocks. At Dunoon (seen in Bullwood Quarry) rocks plunge southeast, but at Strachur they dip northwest. Between the two the rocks gradually flatten out, giving the impression of flat-lying "strata" in Glendaruel and Loch Eckside.

During the crustal collision major dislocations occurred in Central Scotland, the Highland Boundary and Southern Uplands Faults. The Highland Boundary Fault is one of Britain's major structural features crossing Scotland from Stonehaven to Bute, via Loch

GEOLOGICAL MAP OF DUNOON AND COWAL

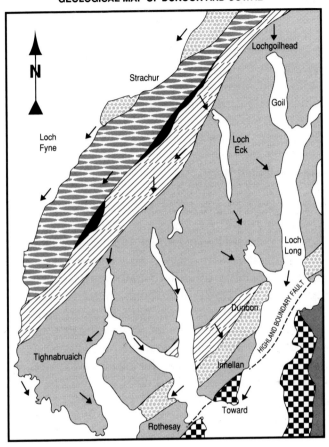

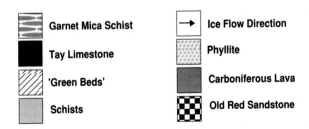

Garnet Mica Schist		Ice Flow Direction	
Tay Limestone		Phyllite	
'Green Beds'		Carboniferous Lava	
Schists		Old Red Sandstone	

Lomond, Kilcreggan, Innellan, Toward and Rothesay Bay. The fault occasionally moves setting off earth tremors, most noticeably at Comrie, Perthshire. Some 450 million years ago the two faults allowed a sinking rift valley to form between them, much like today's East African Rift Valley. Into the valley rivers poured hundreds of metres of red sands and pebbles eroded from the Caledonian Mountains to form Old Red Sandstone. The valley eventually filled up with coal measures and thick flows of lava from volcanic vents like Dumbarton Rock.

During the opening of the Atlantic Ocean 60 million years ago a chain of volcanoes developed in West Scotland, from St Kilda to Arran. From these igneous centres great swarms of dykes were injected into the surrounding, fractured rocks. Cowal was affected by dyke intrusion from the Mull Centre, dykes running northwest to southeast across the area - there are over forty such dykes between Loch Striven and Dunoon. One of the most interesting features forms the prominent hill near Strachur - Sithean Sluaigh, which is an infilled volcanic pipe of this date.

The Ice Age in Cowal

Two million years ago Britain was plunged into a succession of ice advances. Little is known about the early stages, but the last one - the Devensian Ice Age - is well known in West Scotland. The Ice Age developed 25,000 years ago, culminating in a huge ice sheet covering all Scotland 18,000 years ago extending from the Grampians (Rannoch Moor was the breeding centre for the ice) south and west to cover Cowal with some 1,500 metres of ice. As the ice flowed it gouged out deep valleys, polishing and scratching rock surfaces utilising compacted boulders and gravel to erode the bedrocks. The debris pushed ahead and below the ice eventually formed moraines which can be found all over Cowal, but especially in the glens, such as Glen Croe. Some of the boulders carried along by the ice were very large, such as "Jim Crow" at Hunter's Quay. Ice scratches - called striations - are very common - one excellent set occurs in Glen Massan; others can be seen on the Bull Rock pointing south in

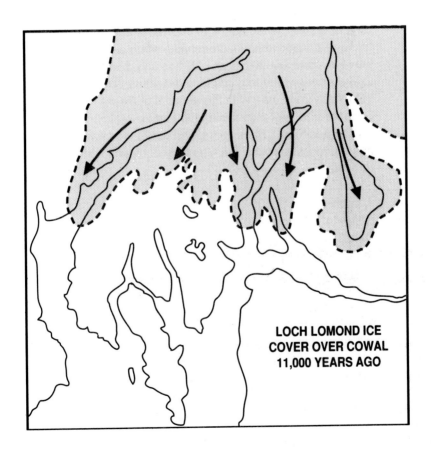

**LOCH LOMOND ICE
COVER OVER COWAL
11,000 YEARS AGO**

the direction of ice movement. *Roches moutonnees* can also be found in Cowal as superb examples of the way ice was able to smooth rocks and pluck them in the same place.

The movement of ice left tell-tale evidence in the form of glacial erratics, usually large boulders picked up by ice in one place and dropped often a long distance away. A good local example is the ice carry of Glen Fyne granite erratics, which can be found all over Cowal. One boulder of this granite can be found at Toward Point, some forty miles from the rock outcrop.

Devensian ice melted about 14,000 years ago returning to the sea water which had been locked up as ice on the land. Sea levels rose quickly flooding many of Cowal's newly formed glens to levels 40 metres higher than today's shores. With the removal of the ice load Scotland lifted up, thus raising the early shorelines as "raised beaches". Such shorelines can be seen at the head of most sealochs, such as Holy Loch and Loch Striven.

Approximately 11,000 years ago there was another ice advance, lasting only a thousand years this time. Called the Loch Lomond Stadial from the excellent terminal features there, the ice sheet reached into North Cowal, ice occupying corries and upper valleys in Glen Croe, Glendaruel, Glen Massan and Glen Lean. The ice melted 10,000 years ago. One of its melting points was on Loch Longside, at Gairletter where there are substantial sands and gravels. Sea levels were 10 - 15 metres higher than now, so raised beaches formed. One of the clearest examples is between Innellan and Toward complete with abandoned cliffs and sea caves.

In the past 10,000 years sea levels have continued to fall with the land adjustment following the complete removal of ice. About 8,000 years ago, however, seawaters flooded back onto the raised beaches with the melting of the North American ice cap. Dunoon town centre is built on a series of raised beach features with a line of old cliffs particularly noticeable from Castle Hill along Argyll Street and round the East and West Bays. Here the post-glacial raised beach is very obvious, but 14,000 years ago all of what is now Dunoon would have been underwater. Even 8,000 years ago seas would have swept the town centre site from the pier to the hospital.

Environment

As the ice receded about 10,000 years ago, the climate in Cowal and the rest of Scotland would have been relatively severe compared to today, and at first only a few very hardy plants could colonise the bare debris. Such plants can be found in Arctic and Alpine regions today, and would have colonised from the south. Lichens were the pioneers, followed by mosses and liverworts, and low growing herbs. On the poor soils slowly formed by these pioneers small shrubs developed such dwarf birch (*Betula nana*) and dwarf willow (*Salix herbacea*). Forests of birch (*Betula pubescens*) followed and later oak (*Quercus petraea*) with rowan (*Sorbus aucuparia*) and holly (*Ilex aquifolia*). On the wet valley bottoms alder (*Alnus glutinosa*) could dominate, as did mixtures of ash *(Fraxinus excelsior)* and wych elm (*Ulmus glabra*) on more fertile and better drained soils. Such woodlands extended up to about 2,000 feet, above which the severity of the climate allowed only moorland plants to grow. The pioneer colonists could only cling on in the north facing corries and on the high tops of mountains, where the competition from other plants is checked by the climate, and some species died out altogether. About 5,000

Scots pine

years ago rainfall increased, leading to waterlogging and washing out of nutrients from the soil. The soils became more acid, inhibiting normal decomposition of plant remains, which then accumulated as peat. On the gentler hills these peat bogs form a complete mantle known as blanket bog.

Animal Arrivals

On the heels of the colonising plants would have come the animals. Again firstly those normally associated with arctic regions: reindeer, giant elk, arctic fox, arctic hare, lemmings, ptarmigan, snow bunting, dotterel, divers, geese and swans. These were followed by more familiar mammals, such as red deer, wolves, lynx and brown bear, and birds such as eagles, peregrines and raven, as the climate allowed. Then, seven or eight thousand years ago the flooding of the English Channel broke the land bridge connection to the continent, and with it Britain's source of land-based colonists. As the climate continued to improve some of the pioneers such as giant elk and lemmings died out, unable to continue their movement northwards. For others, their range moved further north in Scotland, while a few remain confined in Cowal to the high tops and corries in the mountains.

Early Man and Deforestation

It was around this time that early man arrived on the scene. His impact was minimal at first, with small-scale clearing of woodland for grazing and cultivation around the scattered settlements. Deforestation reached a peak in the Middle Ages. Wood was in much demand as building material and fuel, most extravagently to smelt iron in local furnces and bloomeries, eg. Furnace and Newton on Loch Fyne. Trees were also cleared to increase grazing to support an increasing human population.

Agricultural Revolution

By 1800 great expanses of open hillside were used for grazing. Initially cattle and goats were the usual livestock, accompanied by deliberate burning of vegetation to encourage new growth. With the introduction of sheep, grazing pressure increased, and regeneration of natural woodland cover ceased completely. Most flat ground at lower levels was now in cultivation and grazing. Money became the motivation driving land management instead of the subsistence of the people. Communal tenancy farms and the clan system were replaced by Highland estates, during the painful clearances. Several mammal species had already been hunted to extinction, notably lynx, brown bear, beaver, wild boar and wolf. Management of these estates often included some tree planting in "policy woodlands" around the mansion house, leaving us today with some magnificent mature trees at places like Benmore and Ardkinglas. Small leaved lime (*Tilia cordata*), Scots Pine (*Pinus sylvestris*) and Douglas Fir (*Pseudotsuga menziesi*) are particular favourites.

The Forestry Revolution

Following the expedient felling of trees during the Great War, the government of the day realised the value of a strategic reserve. The consequent foundation of the Forestry Commission in 1919 triggered a second period of tree planting on the lower slopes and moorlands. The species used were predominantly for a commercial timber crop, mainly Norway and Sitka Spruce, with some Lodgepole Pine, Scots Pine and Larch. The native hardwoods were even underplanted with conifers in some places, a practice that would be frowned upon today. Those that remained were mostly found on uncultivable, steep, inaccessible or amenity areas, water margins, and as shelter for livestock, and as remnants of oak-hazel coppices once used for charcoal production. For many years the Forestry Commission had the field to themselves, establishing firstly small-holdings (each with a stable), then later forestry villages at Ardentinny, Glenbranter, Deerpark (Benmore) and Glendaruel in order to retain a local workforce.

Many changes have taken place in forestry since the early days. Increasing mechanisation has increased productivity and reduced labour costs. Extraction of timber was once carried out by horses, kept by the workers living in the small-holdings. Now, on easier ground even the felling and removal of side branches can be executed by the same machine, a harvester, which also cuts the timber to length. The timber is then carried off site by a 20 ton 8-wheeled fat-tyred all-wheel-drive vehicle, known as a forwarder, delivering as much as 18 tons to the side of the road at a time. On steeper ground felling is still by chainsaw operators, and extraction is by overhead cable lifting or dragging bundles of logs into stacks at the roadside. Thus the original purpose of the small-holding and its stable no longer exists, and most are now privately owned. Direct labour still has a place but many of the workforce are contractors, not always local residents, and many houses in the forestry villages are also privately owned.

Agricultural Changes

Farming too, has changed much in the 20th century. The large estates no longer function in the same way, if they exist at all. Each estate would once have been made up of several farms, each with a steading based on a previous communal tenancy farm. Now there is often just one farm, the other steadings having been sold. Whereas each mansion would have had a nearby "home farm" and walled garden, supplying the needs of the big house, everyone now shops in the supermarket in Dunoon. Most farms would have had a mixed economy, with some pasture, some arable, some fodder crops and some hill ground, and a range of livestock: sheep, milk cows, beef cattle, horses and maybe pigs. Now many farms have been sold for

dodendron forestry. Some farmers have specialised in sheep, beef or milk, abandoning the mixed economy. Others have

diversified by building holiday accommodation, opening farm shops, or keeping rare breeds for tourists. Milk is still produced for local consumption by a few producer-retailers. However EC milk quotas, beef mountains, foreign imports and cuts in subsidies have made the

35

living of hill farmers ever more precarious, and the future of farming in Cowal is very much under threat.

Plant Life in Cowal

One of the most striking features of the Cowal flora is the variety and abundance of its non-flowering plants - the lichens, liverworts, mosses and ferns. This can attributed to the high rainfall (over a hundred inches per year in the mountainous districts) and the high number of "raindays" when there is some rain, however small. These are conditions that mosses relish, and the peninsula can boast a good list of "Atlantic" seaboard species that are rare on a British scale eg *Plagiochila atlantica.*

The leaching effect of high rainfall combined with the nutrient-poor mica-schist base rock has mainly resulted in infertile acidic soils, especially deficient in phosphate. These are difficult conditions for many plants to grow in, and the vegetation is dominated by those that can cope. With the additional grazing pressure of woolly lawnmowers (sheep) and a burgeoning deer population, the vegetation is nothing like its climax potential. Natural regeneration of native broadleaved woodland (particularly sessile oak, *Quercus petraea*) is very poor, although dense birch scrub (*Betula pubescens*) is able to develop very rapidly on roadside verges. Some highlights do occur where the geology and grazing allows. The series of Tertiary basalt dykes running through Cowal are often lines of weakness exploited by streams to carve out steep-sided and unusually straight ravines. The relatively basic nature of these rocks yield extra nutrients, and in a few places are supplemented by calcium, if the stream cuts though limestone, as in west Glendaruel and Glensluain.

Worthy of particular attention is the fine outcrop of
Serpentine, furnishing a wide range of nutrients, and a
fine show of a plant not found elsewhere in Cowal, the
mountain avens (*Dryas octopetala).*

Mountain and moorland

Much of the upland above the commercial forest is
open moorland. Between 1,800 and 2,200 feet (450
and 650 m) much of Cowal is a rolling, hummocky
plateau covered in a matrix of blanket bog and valley
bog, domain of *Sphagnum* bog mosses, and the bog
cotton grasses (*Eriophorum vaginatum* and *E.
angustifolium*), and which in places has eroded in peat
hags. Drier hummocks are crowned with ling heather
(*Calluna vulgaris*), with cross-leaved heath (*Erica
tetralix*) on the wetter margins.

The steeper, sunny and better drained slopes also have
bell heather (*Erica cinerea*). Where grazing is
particularly heavy the heathers are eliminated
completely and the grass sward is dominated by mat
grass (*Nardus stricta*), and heath rush (*Juncus
squarrosus*), and in damper ground purple moor grass
(*Molinia caerulea*) and the deer sedge (*Trichophorum
cespitosum*). Any deeper, well drained soil is often
colonised by bracken (*Pteridium aquilinum*) and very
wet slopes by sharp-flowered rush (*Juncus acutiflorus*).
Spring colour is provided by the yellow of tormentil
(*Potentilla erecta*) and bog asphodel (*Narthecium
ossifragum*). A brief splash of mauve in June appears in
the flowers of butterwort (*Pinguicula vulgaris*), a

carnivorous plant which can consume small flies in its leaves and thereby supplement the meagre supply of nutrients from the soil.

Above 2,000 feet lies the domain of the low growing Arctic-Alpine plants such as alpine rue (*Thalictrum alpinum*), alpine lady's mantle (*Alchemilla alpina*), and moss campion (*Silene acaulis*). In the corries, high crags and burns can be found roseroot (*Rhodiola rosea*) and several species of saxifrage including yellow (*Saxifraga azoides*) and purple (*S. oppositifolia*). Oases of fertility are centred around the dolerite and basalt dykes, and damp flushes where ground water nutrients concentrate at the surface, giving a much brighter green appearance to the enriched vegetation, which may be extremely varied.

Commercial Forestry

This type of land use has come to dominate nearly the whole of Cowal's landscape in recent decades. Once entirely Forestry Commission owned, the recent growth of private forestry now equals it. In the early decades 50 or 60 years ago, quite a range of conifers were planted including Norway and Sitka spruces, Noble, Douglas and Grand Firs, Western Hemlock, Larches, Lodgepole and Scots Pine. There are even a few stands of Chile Pine (Monkey Puzzle). After this period of experimentation, one species proved to be best suited to conditions in Cowal. The Sitka spruce is the quickest growing, most resistant to deer damage, and has a ready market in pulp mills. It became the forester's favourite, and a phase of planting almost every square metre of plantable ground in the forest was entered. Fortunately attitudes have changed in the last ten years, and all new plantings must now contain at least 5% of broadleaved species. Also planting right up to stream sides is now avoided to reduce water acidification. Other open areas within the forest are much valued by the forest rangers as these clearings tempt deer out for them to gain a clear shot, in order to control their numbers.

Mammals

The largest mammal in Cowal is the Red deer, which although native, had disappeared from the area by the mid nineteenth century, after deforestation and the arrival of sheep farming. Thus when the new forestry plantations were established it was thought unnecessary to erect more than sheep fences around the young trees. However, as the trees grew, so did the number of deer. Today they can inflict so much damage to forestry, especially in young plantations, that six full-time rangers are employed by the Forestry Commission, and over 700 Red deer are shot in a year. Nevertheless, the deer continue to thrive, and will often be spotted in car headlights feeding in fields at night, whilst hiding in the forest by day. Roe deer, too, are common enough to be a pest to forestry and are also culled. They may be observed singly or in twos during a quiet walk along a forest road, especially at dusk and dawn, or seen at night feeding on a roadside verge. A recent imposter in Cowal is the Sika deer, with a stag shot in Strathlachlan in 1975. Sika deer have been at liberty in Knapdale since the First World War and spread up to Inveraray by the 1970s. A hybrid Sik Red stag was shot in Strachur in 1982 and there is a danger

Red deer stag

to the genetic integrity of the Red deer. In the forests
around Lochgilphead the rangers are often hard
pushed to say whether the deer they have shot are one
species or the other since they show features of both.
Sika can normally be told from Red adults by their
spotted pelage in the summer, by their dark, almost
black unspotted coat in winter, and at all times by their
white rather than orange rump patch. Their voice is a

shrieking bark, sometimes accompanied by a grunt, but never the roar like a Red deer.

Brown hares were previously more plentiful, but are now seen less often, probably as a result of changes in land-use ie the lack of arable land. The Mountain hare is occasionally seen on the high hilltops. Unfortunately the Hedgehogs are more often seen dead than alive, killed on roads throughout Cowal, but they still seem to

Red squirrel

be plentiful on lower ground. Cowal has a good
compliment of carnivores. Foxes are not often seen,
being crepuscular and nocturnal, but their distinctive
droppings give them away, and are to be found almost
anywhere. Despite efforts to shoot, snare and poison
them in the name of sheep husbandry they persist,
heard rather than seen, and are most vociferous
between one and three hours after sunset. Elusive too
is the Wildcat, which is rarely encountered in daylight,

in wilder parts of Cowal. The Otter, once widespread, is seen less often than the introduced American mink, which is regularly trapped along the river banks. There are signs that otters are making a comeback, with regular use of spraint (faeces) sites. As yet there are no confirmed sightings of Pine marten, although their range is expanding across Scotland and occur on the other side of Loch Fyne, in Kilmichael Forest. The Badger also seems to be less numerous, but might still be seen out on a nightly forage for its favourite food, juicy earthworms, in a few spots where dairy pasture

Otter

and deciduous woodland meet. To hillwalkers the runs of Short-tailed voles are revealed when snow patches disappear, with the voles themselves scuttling tussocks of grass and rushes. Other small mammals include Wood mice, Bank voles, Common and Pygmy shrews. Red squirrels still exists in a few areas, especially near mature Scots pine trees, and their nests have been found in nestboxes put up for Tawny owls. Grey squirrels don't occur in Cowal yet, and appear less well adapted to conifer woodland than the Red squirrel, but it may only be a matter of time before they invade from Dunbartonshire.

Three species of bat are recorded for Cowal: Pipistrelle, Long-eared and Daubenton's. They probably go unnoticed by many and are certainly under-recorded. Pipistrelles are the ones most likely to be seen patrolling the forest edge just at dusk.

All along the shoreline Common seals are commonly seen, and the Gantock Rocks are a favourite haul out at low tide, just off Dunoon Pier. Toward Point, the Burnt Islands in Kyles of Bute, and the islands in Loch Fyne are all good places to find them. Grey seals also put in an occasional appearance.

Birds

For the ornithologist there is much to offer, with over 100 species of birds breeding in Cowal. The area is well blessed with predators, the largest and most spectacular of which, the Golden eagle, still rears its young in several eyries in the inner glens. Often mistaken for an eagle, the Buzzard is frequently to be seen sitting on telegraph poles or soaring on thermals of hot air, its mewing cry drawing one's attention. Sparrowhawks occur throughout the forests and Kestrel are often seen hovering over moorland searching for an unsuspecting vole. Merlin numbers are low now and they are more likely to be seen during autumn migration. The Hen Harrier is present in most years, the male's pale grey colour with black wing tips appearing deceptively gull-like at first glance. The high population of voles in recently established forest plantations have aided its spread into Cowal after years of absence. Peregrines may be heard screaming regally over inaccessible ledges on their breeding cliffs, waiting for the next racing pigeon to stray in their direction.

The crow family is well represented. The early-nesting Raven frequents the high crags, their eggs hatching in time to feed their youngsters on the eggs of other birds. Rooks are

Golden Eagle

common on the low pastures with several rookeries in Cowal, and some visitors from Rosneath. Magpies, scattered between the glens and around the town, are on the western edge of their range, and are rare elsewhere in Argyll. The Jay's harsh cry is frequent in the woods. The ubiquitous crow is represented by two forms, the all black Carrion Crow and the grey and black Hooded Crow. They can interbreed, producing a complete spectrum of intermediate varieties, which themselves interbreed.

The seashore is an excellent place for finding concentrations of birds and one of the best is the Holy Loch, at the mouth of the river Eachaig. The sand and mud banks can be well viewed from the Kilmun shore, resting one's binoculars on the seawall, or using one's car as a comfortable hide. Five gull species can be seen, and they commute between here and and the Council tip at Dalinlongart. The waders are represented by Curlew, Oystercatcher, Redshank, Lapwing, and Ringed Plover feeding on the abundance of invertebrates in the mud exposed by the ebb tide. Bar-tailed Godwits and Greenshank put in seasonal appearances during migration. Wildfowl too are attracted to the convergence of fresh and salt water. Mallard, Wigeon and Teal feed on the grass at high tide. A couple of pairs of Shelduck breed in burrows in the saltmarsh creeks. Eider assemble in rafts offshore, diving down to collect mussels and periwinkles from the sea bed. In the river itself, the Red-breasted Merganser are joined in winter months by Goldeneye and Little Grebe, and in summer by Common sandpiper and the occasional Goosander.

Along the water's edge, both fresh and salt, the Heron stands sentinel, waiting for its prey to stray within stabbing distance. Nowhere in Cowal are the heronries large, maybe up to 5 or 6 pairs, and often in conifer trees making them very hard to observe.

Up and down the rivers flies the Dipper, also an early nester, building its dome-shaped home in March, and beneath the arch of a bridge or roots of a tree are favourite sites. Pied wagtails are more common than the yellow breasted Grey wagtail. Nesting in a colony of holes in river banks and somewhat perilously in sand quarries, the Sand Martin breeds in a few localities. The Kingfisher is a delightful visitor, on the edge of its range, and most records are in late summer and probably represent juvenile dispersal from the Clyde catchment.

In spring the woodlands come alive with birdsong, especially areas of mixed hardwood, eg. Glenbranter, Lochgoilhead and Caladh. Besides the more familiar birds of gardens are Wood Warbler, Willow Warbler Flycatchers are regular arrivals in May, and are now joined by small numbers of Pied Flycatchers, of which the handsome black and white male arrives before the brown and white female. The Great Spotted Woodpecker widely advertises his presence by hammering on branches. The yaffle call of the Green Woodpecker is sometimes heard although its not yet a regular breeder. Tawny Owls are still common, but the Barn Owl is declining. Short-eared Owls have benefited in a similar way to Hen harriers. On the forest edge the Tree Pipit flutters upwards warbling its proclamation of ownership.

Moving out to the southwest of Cowal, some very pleasant walks can be had along the coast. In the low scrub of bramble, gorse and small trees, the Stonechat, Grasshopper Warbler and Whitethroat sing. Out on the heathland the Snipe drum overhead at dusk, and with luck a Nightjar may be heard churring its nocturnal song during high summer.

Reptiles and Amphibians

Adders and Common Lizards are rare, found on dry heathland. Slow worms are more common, often sheltering in the cool under large rocks. From February into March frog spawn is abundant, especially in the ditches beside forest roads. Toads are also present as is the palmate newt.

Fish and fishing

Angling takes place on river, loch and sea, for salmon, sea and brown trout. Some of the lochans are stocked with rainbow trout e.g. Loch Loskin. Mackerel are an easy catch in the summer, and the cod used to be quite sizeable.

Two fish require special mention. Loch Eck boasts a sub-species of charr (*Salvelinus alpinus youngeri*) found nowhere else, and a species of freshwater herring known as powan (*Coregonus laveretus clupeoides*) elsewhere found only in Loch Lomond. The presence of these two species, along with trout and salmon, render the fish community in Loch Eck unique, now that the introduction of ruffe into Loch Lomond has altered the ecological relationships of the fish there. This was a major reason why Loch Eck is now designated a Site of Special Scientific Interest in 1991, by the Nature Conservancy Council for Scotland.

This brief survey covers a great deal of ground and, though wide ranging, is far from comprehensive. The distribution of all vertebrates is being mapped by the Clyde area branch of the Scottish Wildlife Trust, while the Argyll Bird Report records the birds seen in Cowal. Much remains to be discovered about Cowal's wildlife, and any interesting or unusual records should be sent to Cowal Natural History Society c/o Ardentinny Centre, Ardentinny, by Dunoon, Argyll, PA23 8TR.

Placenames

Dunabhainn

Comghall

Just as the Inuit have a hundred words for snow and the Arabs a hundred words for sand, so Gaelic has a lot of words meaning hill. An oft quoted verse begins:

A mountain's a mountain in England, but when
The climber's in Scotland it may be a beinn,
or a creag or a meall, a spidean, a sgòr,
a càrn or a monadh, a stuc or a tòrr".

The place names of Cowal are fairly typical of much of the rest of the country's names in that they consist of those which can be explained with reasonable certainty and those which cannot, although there is never any shortage of suggestions for the latter. Generally, but not always, place names contain more than one element, and while we may know what one part of a name means, another part may elude us.

Dunoon, the main town in Cowal, provides a good example of this. This word has had over forty different spellings at one time or another, and almost as many suggested meanings. This is, no doubt, an extreme example, but such uncertainties appear regularly throughout Cowal. Even today many place names in the peninsula are spelt in slightly different ways and atlases often do not agree on a standard form.

With regard to different spellings, earlier forms may often give a clue to the meaning of a word. A good example is Ardachuple, a farm at the head of Loch Riddon. Fifteenth century and later sources give the form Ardaphubil, or similar, meaning the height or promontory of the tent (Gaelic *pubull;* English pavilion). The reference is to a tent or pavilion erected there by Sir Colin Campbell to entertain visitors from Ireland. Another instance is Finbracken in Sandbank. Pont's map of Cowal (c.1600) gives Finbacken, which suggests the meaning fair banks, although the Gaelic *bac*, a bank, is borrowed from Norse and usually reflects a Viking presence. In this and other names in Cowal an earlier form of the word may one day shed more light.

While most, by far, of the place names in the peninsula are Gaelic, there may be a pre-Gaelic instance in Loch Long on the eastern boundary of Cowal. Ptolemy, writing in Greek in the second century AD, mentions a river Longos, but its identification with Loch Long is uncertain. Loch Long is usually taken to mean ship loch; the Gaelic word *long*, a ship, is assumed to have been borrowed from Latin (*navis*) *longa*, a long ship or warship, which does no harm to the chronology.

Gaelic place names, however, dominate. This reflects the settlement of the area by Gaelic speaking Scots from Ireland from around 500 AD onwards, who brought, with Columba and others, the Christianity of the Celtic church. Consequently there are a number of

Kils in Cowal. Kil (Gaelic *cill;* English cell) refers to a
monastic cell or the site of an early church. The best
known are Kilmun, the church of St Mun (various
spellings), a follower of St Columba; Kilfinan, on Loch
Fyne, the church of St Finan, a name given to several
early Celtic saints; and Kilmodan, the church of St
Modan. St Catherines, near Strachur, was formerly Cill
Catrine, a church dedicated to St. Catherine of
Alexandria.

The Gaelic word *dùn*, a hill, hillfort, (English down)
appears in Dunoon; the meaning of the second part is
uncertain. The current favourite seems to be river,
(Gaelic *abhainn*), although the pronunciation of the
Gaelic form of the word - *Dunomhainn* - does not
support this. *Dùn* was also adopted by the Victorians;
hence the large mansions and grounds of Dunselma,
Strone (Selma was a Fingalian palace in Argyll) and
Dunclutha, Kirn (*Clutha* is the River Clyde, *Clota* to the
Romans).

Aird, a height or promontory, is another common root,
usually taking the form *ard* in compounds. So
Ardentinny is the height of the fire (Gaelic *teine*); the
fire may have been used to signal for a ferry across
Loch Long, or as a sign of approaching danger.
Ardlamont is the promontory of the Lamonts. Lamont is
the anglicised form of the Gaelic *Laomunn*, itself from
Norse *Lagman*, a law-man - stress on the first syllable.
These Lamonts later became part of Clan Lamont, the
main Cowal clan. Another name of Norse origin,
Lachlan, appears in Strathlachlan, the ancestral lands
of Clan MacLachlan. *Lochlann* - (sea) loch land - is the
general Gaelic term for Scandinavia.

Ardnadam, near Sandbank, is another "height", but of

what? The picture is further complicated by the existence of two pronunciations, one with the stress on the second or middle, syllable, the other with the stress on the last syllable. This latter is explained by the Gaelic word *damh*, an ox, or a sage. Those who favour "the height of the oxen", or "the height of the learned men", however, have to explain why the word remains unaspirated (*dam*) contrary to the normal Gaelic experience. Barr na Damh near Tighnabruaich is only one of several Cowal place names which show the usual form. (*Bàrr* means upland, high ground, rather like *àird*.) This suggests, then, that the pronunciation with the stress on the second or middle syllable may be correct, with a reference to one Adam, of uncertain identity.

Inver, a confluence or river mouth, appears in several places, as Inverchaolain, the mouth of the narrow river, on Loch Striven. The other part of the word contains the word *caol,* often anglicised as kyle. *Caol* appears again in Colintraive (*caol an t-snàimh*, the narrows of the swimming) the swimming being done by cattle between Cowal and Bute at that point. Nearby is Ardentraive, the height of the swimming. Another *inver* is Inverchapel, the confluence of the horses, from Gaelic *capull*, horse (English, cavalry). This area at the south end of Loch Eck has a traditionally strong connection with horses. Loch Eck itself is the horse loch, from Gaelic *each,* horse. (English equine, etc.)

Another important Gaelic place name root is *creag*, with the related form *carraig*, both meaning rock (English crag). Carraig Castle, on the shore of Loch Goil, is built on a prominent rock. Creggans (rocks) near Strachur is an example of an erroneous and unnecessary English plural; *-an* is the Gaelic plural ending. Another related

Gaelic word, *càrn*, a heap of stones, a cairn, is found in Cairndow, the black (*dubh*) cairn, at the head of Loch Fyne.

Other important place names of Gaelic origin are - Tighnabruaich, the house on the hill; Strachur, the *strath* (valley) of the heron (Gaelic *corra*); nearby is Loch nan Corra, the Heron Loch. Strone, a point, is at the foot of Loch Long; Stronsaul, in Glen Kin denotes a ridge (of barns, probably, Gaelic *sabhal*). Both meanings are from Gaelic *sròn*, a nose. A similar idea occurs in Succoth, near Strachur, and elsewhere, from *soc*, a snout, used of a point of land jutting between two rivers. Blairmore is the big field *(blàr*, a field, and *mór*, big), rather like Auchamore, now a part of Dunoon. The common adjective *mór* occurs again at Benmore, the big hill, and Ballimore, the big farm. Kames is *camus*, a bay; Camusreinach, bracken bay, was an old name of Hunter's Quay. Lettermay, near Lochgoilhead, contains the common Gaelic root *leitir*, a slope, hillside; here it denotes a sloping field (*magh*, a field). Similarly Gairletter on Loch Long is the short slope (*geàrr*, short, or cut).

Among the glens in Cowal are Glen Croe, the glen of the cattle enclosure (Gaelic *crò*); Glen Lean, the broad glen (Gaelic *leathan*); Glen Kin, the narrow glen (Gaelic *cumhang*); and Glen Tarsan, the across, or transverse, glen (Gaelic *tarsuinn*); it cuts across Glen Lean and Glen Massan. Glendaruel, famous in history and song, is a much corrupted form probably meaning the glen of the red river, from the colour of the surrounding soil. c.f. *Caol ruadh*, the red kyle, near Colintraive.

The most widely known hill is the Cobbler, generally

thought to mean the forked mountain, from Gaelic *gobhal*. The letter "b" sound in English Cobbler, however, is unlikely to have arisen from an attempt to reproduce the Gaelic, for the aspirated b of the latter is silent. Scots provides a good illustration of this with horny-golloch, from Gaelic *gobhlachan*, an earwig. Thus Loch Goil, forking off Long Long, is more likely to contain *gobhal*. The Cobbler is also known as Ben Arthur, although whether this is a reference to Clan MacArthur or to the legendary King Arthur is uncertain. Cowal also has a few fairy hills (Gaelic *sithean*) the best known being Sithean Sluaigh, near Strachur, the fairy hill of the (fairy) folk.

Cowal itself has had no shortage of meanings attributed to it, but the generally accepted view is that the name goes back to the sixth century to *Comghall,* the grandson of Fergus Mór, leader of the first Scots to enter Argyll.

There are few names of Norse origin in Cowal in contrast to other parts of Argyll, particularly the islands. There are, of course, a number of small islands off the Cowal coast, especially on the west side. Significantly, they do not contain the ending -*ay*, (Norse for island) which is common further west in Argyll, but mainly feature the Gaelic *eilean* (island). Innellan is thought to contain the element *eilean*, referring to an off-shore rock there called the Perch. This rock is much frequented by birds, which some have thought strengthens the probability that the Gaelic *eun* (bird) is the first part of the word. If Innellan means "bird island" we would normally expect the stress to be on the first part of the name, but local pronunciation is sometimes unusual in these matters, as, for example, the current pronunciation of the name Sandbank, with the stress on the second syllable, indicates. However, the main problem is that Innellan is not an island, and we would expect at least some reference to the mainland. Island farm, on Loch Eck, for instance, is on the mainland, but is named after a nearby small islet in the loch.

The Vikings do not seem to have spent too long in Cowal, no doubt discouraged by their defeat at Glendaruel. So, although we find in Cowal places such as Feorlinn (farthing land), Lephinchapel (half-penny land of the horses) and Lephinmore (big half-penny land) with their references to the Norse system of land measurement, the system was, of course, taken over and extended by the Gaels. So the word "seat", in the Bishop's Seat, a hill near Dunoon, or in the nearby Horse Seat, is unlikely to be from Norse *setr*, a dwelling or shieling. *Setr* names are not found in mainland Argyll.

Sea lochs, of course, are a feature of Cowal, and the Vikings were certainly frequent visitors to these waters. Loch Long was called Skipfiord (ship fiord) by them. Well known also is the raid up Loch Long in 1263 by a Norse fleet, with the assistance of some Gaels, to Arrochar. At nearby Tarbet they dragged their ships across the narrow stretch of land (which is what the common name *Tarbe*(r)*t* means) to Loch Lomond.

One Norse name in Cowal is Ormidale (snake dale) at the head of Loch Riddon. Another, Altgaltrig, on the Kyles of Bute, may contain the Norse word for boar. The Gaelic first part of the word, *allt*, is stream, so, here we have the stream of the boar. There are at least fifty stream names in Cowal, referring to horses, cattle,

sheep, deer, polecats and otters. Ascog Bay, the bay
of the ash trees, also looks Norse (Norse *sk* = English
sh, as in *skip*/ship above). All these places border the
sea.

It is interesting to notice a new stratum of English
names appearing in the continuing history of Cowal.
Some of these are translations, such as St Catherines,
Rashfield, Whistlefield (partly) and Holy Loch. This last
appears in Pont's map as Loch Aint, presumably a
misunderstanding of the aspirated form of *seunta*
(sacred, charmed) - English sign (of the cross), - the
Gaelic name of the loch. Others replace earlier names,
as Sandbank, formerly Claddyhouse (shore house). A
sandbank (Gaelic *oitir*) is also found in Otter Ferry on
Loch Fyne. The resurgence of the area in Victorian
times is reflected in names such as Hunter's Quay, part
of the lands of Hafton bought by James Hunter in the
nineteenth century, and Graham's Point, at Kilmun.

Times Past

From a glance at the map, the Cowal Peninsula looks like a three pronged mass hanging over the Island of Bute. The interior of Cowal is scored with long narrow lochs and the roads bend and twist as they go round the heads of lochs or follow their indented shores. Fifteen miles as the crow flies may well become eighty miles as the car follows the twisting roads. Yet what is now seen as a barrier to easy travel is the key to the settlement of Cowal in the past. When travel was almost entirely by water, in order to avoid boggy low ground, steep rocky slopes and wild animals such as wolves and wild boar, Cowal with its wealth of lochs and rivers was an easy place to settle.

The First Inhabitants

When the ice retreated at the end of the Ice Age a scanty vegetation began to appear and in time animals came to browse on it. Their presence attracted the wandering hunters of the Mesolithic period, who probably came north only in the summers, returning farther south as the cold winters approached. Their temporary camp sites were marked only by the middens, heaps of shells and bones of small animals, which they left behind them. More permanent sites which were established later have been recognised near Oban and in Bute. It seems more than likely that such settlements would have existed in Cowal, although none has yet been found.

We are on surer ground with the first real settlers, the Neolithic farmers. Their culture, based on tilling the ground and rearing animals, rather than on hunting and food-gathering, meant that they formed permanent settlements. The farming methods, using a "slash and burn" technique for clearing the ground in order to grow barley and corn, were wasteful, exhausting the fertility of the soil and rendering it unproductive. In addition a settled life brought about an increase in population, as both the young and the old were more likely to survive. This meant that new areas had to be cleared and brought under cultivation.

Gradually they spread over the whole country, living in family groups in huts made of wood and turf. Naturally, these have disappeared in the course of time and are recognisable only by the evidence of blackened hearths and post holes which once held the wooden uprights of their houses. Two such sites have been excavated by Cowal Archaeological Society. One was on a hillside in Glendaruel at Achategan, and the other at Ardnadam, near Loch Loskin. In both cases the Neolithic site was revealed only after going down through the layers of a number of successive occupations. However, if their houses are impermanent, the final resting places of their dead are not. They built huge communal tombs,

Adam's grave near Sandbank

with an inner chamber made of upright stone slabs (megaliths), covered by a great capstone, the whole then hidden under a huge mound of stones. These cairns may have been as much as 100 feet long, covering a burial chamber perhaps only 15 feet in length. There is some evidence that the final layer on the cairn may have been of white quartzite pebbles, making the great tomb a landmark for miles around. Over the millennia since they were constructed most of the cairns have been robbed of their stone for road-making or dyke-building, leaving the great megaliths exposed. There are two very good examples in Cowal; Adam's Grave, near Sandbank, and Ach-na-ha, near the Otter Ferry-Kilfinan road.

The discovery of the use of metal was an important development. Copper was the first to be used, although it is too soft for much more than decorative use, but it was greatly improved by mixing it with tin to produce the alloy bronze. One of the most important centres in the British Isles of these bronze-using people was at Kilmartin, near Lochgilphead, on the western side of Loch Fyne, where there is an impressive array of cairns and standing stones to attest to their presence. It is not surprising that the eastern shores of Loch Fyne should also show clearly the presence of Bronze Age farmers.

Unlike the Neolithic people with their great communal tombs, these people buried their dead in single graves. They placed them, in a crouched position, in a cist (a stone-sided box), covered it with a lid of stone and then built a large round cairn of stones above it. There are a number of these cairns at Kilfinan, an impressive one near the ferry terminal at Colintraive, and several at Portavadie, some of which were destroyed when the ground was cleared for a planned oil-rig building site which was never used. Other enigmatic traces of the presence of these long gone people are single or grouped standing stones, which may be the remnants of stone circles, smaller versions of Brodgar in Orkney or Callanish in Lewis. There are also boulders or rock faces covered with cup marks, indented shallow holes in the rock. Occasionally they are surrounded by circles or linked to each other by grooves carefully incised on the rock. The work must have been tedious and exacting but important - but we cannot understand or decipher it. Various explanations have been put forward. One is that the cups may have a ritual significance, representing the eyes of a goddess, as to us a cross represents Christianity. Another is that they may have marked boundaries between tribes or families, or that they may have some connection with copper mining.

The Coming of the Celts

The bronze-using period was to give way gradually to what is called the Iron Age. By about 200 BC the use of iron for tools and weapons was almost universal, although copper, bronze and occasionally gold were used for personal decoration. Successive waves of immigrant peoples arrived in the British Isles, bringing with them a new way of living. One of the most important influences on the history of Europe at this period was the great expansion of the Celtic peoples from their original homelands in Austria and Switzerland. They swept across Europe settling and colonising. The first wave to reach these islands spoke a Celtic language which still remains in Welsh and

Cornish, which are closely allied to Breton in France. The second great wave settled in what is now Ireland, speaking a language, Gaelic, which is the official language of Eire. It was from Northern Ireland that a tribe of these people, known as the Scotti, crossed to the West of Scotland, eventually giving their name to the whole country. They established themselves in Argyll *(Earra-ghaidheal* - the land of the Gaels).

A great deal is known about the Celtic peoples, partly from their own tales and legends, and partly from the reports sent home by Roman Generals and historians who encountered and fought against the Celts in many of their campaigns in Europe.

They were a proud and warlike people with a strongly defined culture, based on a hierarchical structure of warriors, farmers and slaves. Their priests, the Druids, were also historians and keepers of the laws and received a long and arduous training in their duties. This training was essential as the Celts were non-literate, and their highly complex literature, history and laws were preserved in oral tradition only. Poets and musicians were held in high regard in this rich barbaric culture, which delighted equally in feats of strength and agility. The Celts loved colour and ornament, wearing cloaks of crimson, saffron or green, with rich brooches to hold them on the shoulder. Chieftains wore neck torques and arm bands of gold to mark their status, and were expected to display courage in battle and hospitality in their great halls. Celtic art was so individual and easily recognisable that it is still copied and you may well find souvenirs in the form of jewellery of Celtic design or articles with the intricate, interlacing motifs so characteristic of the art of this fascinating culture. Their language survives in Gaelic, spoken until comparatively recently in Cowal and still evident in the placenames of the peninsula.

One of the most interesting relics from this period is the Glen Massan manuscript, now in the National Library of Scotland. It was found in a house in Glen Massan, near Sandbank, and is thought to be of 13th century date. It is written in Scottish Gaelic, but tells one of the great stories of Ireland, the story of Deirdre of the Sorrows, who fled to Scotland with her lover and his brothers, to escape the wrath of the High King of Ireland, who sought to marry her. The poem tells of their wanderings in Argyll and contains her famous lament for lost happiness as they are tricked into returning to Ireland and the tragic fate that awaits them.

The name "Cowal" is said to derive from *Comgall,* one of the leaders of the Scotti who settled in Argyll in the 5th century. To defend their lands they fortified suitable sites such as hill tops, tidal islets, or peninsulas and headlands, with ditches and ramparts which enclosed groups of timber huts. Those *"duns"* have given their name to many sites and Dunoon itself derives its name from the Celtic *dun* which occupied what is now known as the Castle Hill. The name may mean "The fort by the river" *(Dun-obhainn)* or "The fort of strangers" *(Dun-oidhean).* Other notable "duns" are the magnificent Barr Iola, near Otter Ferry; Barmore, commanding the entrance to Glendaruel; and Inverglen, near Strachur.

The Early Christian Church

Christianity came to Scotland with St Ninian who

established his church, known as Candida Casa (the white house) at Whithorn in Galloway. From this base he and his followers set out on long missionary journeys which led to the foundation of Christian churches in many places in Scotland. It is possible that he or one of his monks came to Cowal, but there is no firm evidence of this.

Ireland, however, had been Christianised by missionaries from Wales and, of course, by the famous St Patrick, who may have come from Scotland. There was a thriving monastic tradition which was very well suited to the way of life of the Celtic clan. There was already a close relationship between Ireland and the West of Scotland, and it was natural that when Columcille, of royal birth and a noted cleric, was exiled from Ireland for his defiance of the High King, he should cross to Argyll. With his twelve companions to help him set up a monastery, he searched for a suitable site. King Aedan of the Scots, granted him the little island of Iona off the south west coast of Mull. Iona was to become one of the great religious centres of Europe, and still attracts thousands of pilgrims and visitors each year.

Columba, as he was now known, was a man of enterprise and energy. He and his monks set out on ambitious missionary journeys. Indeed the first recorded sighting of a monster in Loch Ness is reported in Adamnan's "Life of St. Columba".

Monks of the Celtic Church came to Cowal and established many chapels. These were small and simple buildings intended for the use of the priest alone. Near the chapel would be a mound with a preaching cross on it round which people would gather, and also a simple hut where the monk would live. Some of these chapels have completely disappeared, leaving evidence of their presence only in place-names with the prefix "Kil" (from *cill* - a chapel), as in Kilbride, in Dunoon, and Kilfinan. Some early chapels were incorporated into later medieval churches. An example of this may be in Strachur, where the present church is within a circular enclosure which is typically Celtic, and at Kilmun, where there was a very early site, now hidden by a medieval tower and a later church. At Kilmodan, in Glendaruel, where there is no vestige of the early chapel, there is a fine collection of medieval grave stones, with another fine group in a vault near the church at Kilfinan. The Church of the Three Brethren, at Lochgoilhead, is an interesting building and its dedication would suggest that it is a very early Christian site, although no one knows the origin of its unusual name. Excavations at Ardnadam, near Loch Loskin, revealed an early chapel with a rough stone altar.

The Vikings

In ancient Norway a man's possessions were divided on his death among all his heirs. This resulted in the establishment of small farms which, after a few generations, were too small to yield a living. Many younger men sold their shares to other members of their families and set off to win wealth by raiding or settling elsewhere. An added attraction was that "sword-wealth" was a man's to dispose of as he liked. At first the Norse attacks were "hit and run" affairs. They soon realised where their task would be easy. The sacred Isle of Iona was raided three times in ten years, and other monastic establishments were wont to pray, "From the fury of the Norsemen, Good Lord deliver us".

Gradually the Norsemen began to settle, and by the 10th century the Northern Isles of Shetland and Orkney and much of the Hebrides had come under Norse domination, as can be seen by their placenames. An agreement had been arrived at with the King of Scots, whereby the Norsemen could claim land they could sail round, with the obvious intention of restricting them to the islands. This led to a famous incident when the longships of Magnus Barelegs were dragged across the narrow neck of land between Tarbert, Loch Fyne, and West Loch Tarbert, thus claiming the whole of the peninsula of Kintyre as Norse.

As yet no definitely Norse settlements have been found in Cowal although the name Ormidale on Loch Riddon is very much a Norwegian name. One Viking at least must have settled down to farm peacefully in this sheltered spot.

Norwegian ships certainly cruised up the sea lochs that reach into the heart of Argyll. In 1110 a fleet of longships beached on the Otter Spit in Loch Fyne. Tradition states that there were so many that the crews could reach the Cowal shore by leaping from ship to ship. The local people gathered and a fierce battle was fought in Glendaruel. It is said that the river ran red with blood before the remaining Norsemen were driven back to their ships.

In 1263 King Haakon of Norway mustered a large fleet which sailed up the Clyde, into Loch Long and up to the head of the loch. Some of the ships were dragged on rollers across the short distance to Loch Lomond.

There they were launched again to harry the islands and shores of the Loch. The longships then sailed down the River Leven to the Clyde, thus repeating the stratagem that had worked so well in Kintyre.

Later that year, however, King Haakon's great fleet was defeated at Largs by a combination of storms and the dogged resistance of the Scots. In 1266 the Norse Kings relinquished all their claims to the Western Highlands and Islands, retaining only Orkney and Shetland.

The Medieval Period

When Alexander III of Scotland died tragically in 1286, his two-year-old granddaughter, Margaret, the Maid of Norway, was recognised as his heir. When she too died only four years later on her way from her home in Norway to Scotland, the country was plunged into disorder. There were a number of claimants to the throne and Edward I of England offered to act as "an honest broker". Predictably he chose weak-willed John Balliol who would be a puppet king. The Scots called him "Toom Tabard" - empty coat. When at last Balliol rebelled against Edward, he was forced to flee. Edward gave up any pretence, led his army into Scotland and occupied the principal towns and castles. A popular uprising led by Sir William Wallace had some success but Wallace was captured and executed. Throughout this troubled period the clans of the west took little part in events. Argyll was virtually independent and the clan leaders were interested mainly in furthering their own personal ambitions.

When another of the claimants, Robert Bruce, was crowned King against Edward's wishes he did not have universal support. His small army was defeated and Bruce fled. Two important clans, the MacDougalls in Lorn and the Lamonts in Cowal had supported Balliol and remained adherents of the English side. Although this must have seemed to them a prudent policy at the time, it was in the end disastrous. After Bruce's great victory at Bannockburn in 1314 he rewarded Sir Neil Campbell of Lochawe, who had been his loyal supporter from the beginning, with lands taken from the MacDougalls and the Lamonts. The principal clans in Cowal were now the Lamonts, Campbells, MacLachlans, MacNaughtons and the MacEwens.

A generation later, John Balliol's son, Edward, claimed the throne and with English support was crowned at Scone, while Bruce's young son fled to France. Balliol's army swept through Scotland and among other successes captured Dunoon Castle in 1334. This castle, one of the earliest stone castles in Scotland, held a commanding position on the Firth of Clyde. A small force of 400 men, under Sir Colin Campbell, who was loyal to the Bruce dynasty, attacked and regained the castle. Tradition says that the local people joined in the attack, running to the shore and hurling stones at the boats as the defeated English soldiers made their escape. In 1337 Dunoon Castle became a Royal Palace and in 1469 an Act was passed that the "Castle of Dunnune" should in all time coming be the property of the heir to the Scottish throne. In 1472 a Royal Charter made Colin Campbell, Count of Argyll, the Hereditary Keeper of the Castle. He was to present a red rose as rent when required.

The most famous Royal visitor to the castle was Mary,

Queen of Scots, who stayed there for three days while making a Royal Progress in the West. She and her entourage had stayed in Inveraray, where her half-sister was Countess of Argyll, then crossed by ferry to Creggans near Strachur, spending the night at Driep. Next day she rode to Dunoon. While there she held court and extended royal clemency to some freebooters and watched an archery contest at the Butts, where McColl's Hotel is now situated. She left to visit Toward Castle, seat of the Lamonts, before crossing the Firth to tour South West Scotland.

In 1958 her successor, the present Queen Elizabeth, visited Dunoon and was presented with a red rose by the Captain of Dunstaffnage, deputising for the Duke of Argyll, Hereditary Keeper of the Castle.

Very little remains of the castle. It fell into disrepair as its importance faded and was plundered for its stone, most notably by Mr Ewing who used the stone to build a wall round his new estate. Later what was left was flattened to make a platform for guns and searchlights in two World Wars. What had been the bailey or outerworks of the original castle was transformed into the modern Castle Gardens. It requires an effort of will and imagination to ignore the flower beds and putting greens and replace them with stables, blacksmiths and men at arms.

Another smaller Campbell castle is Knockamillie, on the hill behind Innellan. Only a fragment remains but it makes a dramatic picture against the waters of the Firth.

The Lamont Clan had retained their lands in South Cowal and their castles at Ascog and Toward can still be seen, though Ascog Castle is ruinous and dangerous. Toward Castle has a fine tower with one wall collapsed and a later hall-house which was excavated in recent years. Its entrance gateway is especially fine.

Castle Lachlan is a dramatic ruin standing in a fine position on a rocky promontory on the east shore of Loch Fyne. The modern Castle Lachlan stands a short distance away.

One of the finest castles in Cowal is Carrick Castle, on Loch Goil. This is an impressive Keep, dating from the 15th century. It was originally a Lamont castle, but passed in the early 16th century into the possession of the Campbells.

Clan Rivalry

After the Union of the Crowns in 1603, the importance of the royal castles declined. The King and his court departed from Edinburgh to London and the West was even further away from the centre of power. The old ways of living continued, farming and fishing being the principal occupations of the local people. Rivalry among the clans also continued, occasionally coming to a head with raids and reprisals.

The most serious of these took place in 1646. Charles I had been defeated by an alliance of English Parliamentarians (Roundheads) and Scots Presbyterians who resented Charles's attempts to force Episcopalianism on the Church of Scotland in his wish to control the Kirk by appointing its Bishops. The

Carrick Castle

powerful Campbell clan supported the Presbyterian
cause and the Earl of Argyll signed the National
Covenant, pledging to resist the King's encroachments.
After the execution of Charles I, which was against the
wishes of his Scottish opponents, an attempt was made
to instal his son on the throne of Scotland. The Marquis
of Montrose, a brilliant soldier, led the supporters of the
new King, while the Earl of Argyll, fearing a resumption
of attempts to force Bishops on the Church of Scotland,
led the Presbyterian army. Civil war had broken out.
After a campaign in Northeast Scotland Montrose led
his army on an astounding march in mid-winter through
mountain passes choked with snow, to attack Inveraray
itself, the capital of Argyll. This surprise attack was
successful. There was time only to send the women
and children across Loch Fyne to safety in Strachur.
The town was looted and set on fire and those who
escaped fled to the hills.

The chief of the Lamont clan, most probably motivated
by hostility to the Campbells and the hope of acquiring
more land should the King be successful, led his
clansmen to join Colkitto and his Irishmen who were
Montrose's allies. They were engaged in harrying the
rest of Argyll.

Eventually the Lamonts left Colkitto and set off for
home. On their way they attacked and burned the
house of Campbell of Ardkinglas despite the fact that
Campbell was the brother-in-law of the Lamont chief.
They then attacked Strachur, possibly because the
people there had given shelter to the refugees from
Inveraray. The official records of Clan Lamont tell of
the slaughter of 33 people in Strachur and the
destruction of their homes and possessions. The
Lamonts moved on to Glenbranter where the

inhabitants had fled, leaving behind only one old man who was paralysed. He was stripped naked and taken outside to die. The next attack was on Kilmun on the shores of the Holy Loch. The people had taken refuge in the church but were lured out by the promise of safe conduct. The promise was immediately broken, the people were massacred on the shore, with the exception of one man who was actually killed in the church, since he was, as the records say, "in the hot fever" and they feared to touch him.

Campbell revenge was swift. Toward Castle was besieged by a force led by Campbell of Ardkinglas. The siege was protracted and eventually the defenders were offered safe conduct if they came out and surrendered. Like the earlier Lamont offer at Kilmun this was dishonoured, although the Campbells did send the women and children to safety across the Firth. The Lamont chief, his brother and their immediate families were imprisoned in Dunstaffnage Castle, near Oban. The other members of the clan, however, were shown little mercy. They were taken by boat from Toward to Dunoon and at the Hill of Justice on Tom-a-mhoid Road (where there now stands a memorial) they were sentenced to death. They were hanged from a tree standing in front of the High Kirk of Dunoon, now called the Old Parish and St. Cuthbert's. Among their number was the Provost of Rothesay who was unlucky enough to be visiting his relatives in Toward Castle when the siege began.

A romantic, though macabre, story was told that the tree never bore leaves again and that when it was eventually cut down, the roots gushed blood. For many years this has seemed only a fanciful and rather gruesome tale, but recently a rich vein of iron oxide has been noted in that spot. In water this certainly looks like blood.

The most romantic part of the story was yet to come. Among the women allowed to go in safety was the Chief's sister, Lady Isobel. She had kept the written promise of safe conduct, folded it into a long narrow spill and braided it into her hair so that it was completely hidden. In later years when Charles II did regain the throne, she was able to produce the letter, tell of the sufferings of her clan in the King's cause, and claim compensation. This marked the virtual end of Campbell power in Cowal.

In 1685 the 9th Earl of Argyll brought a small force from Holland to invade Scotland in support of Monmouth's rising in the West of England against James VII and II. Argyll's army landed at Loch Riddon and after several local skirmishes marched along the shore of Loch Eck and crossed over the Larach pass to Ardentinny, from where they crossed by boat to Coulport. The ill-fated expedition met its end in Dunbartonshire and Argyll himself was captured at Inchinnan. He was later tried and beheaded in Edinburgh. Savage reprisals followed this abortive rising and local tradition states that valuable documents belonging to the Argyll family were concealed in a cave on the hillside above Loch Eck. The cave has since been known as the Paper Cave.

Campbell land in Dunoon was sold to one MacArthur, the local miller, who became Laird of Milton. His handsome house can be seen in Milton Avenue, at the top of Ferry Brae. It is now local government offices.

18th Century Developments.

After the failure of Prince Charles Edward Stuart's
Rising in 1745, the disaster of Culloden and the
attempts at genocide by "Butcher" Cumberland and his
men, the Highlands suffered terribly. Argyll escaped
this as the Earl of Argyll, loyal to his Presbyterian
beliefs, had not been among the supporters of the
Prince and indeed many of those fleeing from the
Government troops found shelter in Argyll.

Farming was the main occupation of the people. A
small group of houses formed a "clachan" and both
work and recreation were communal. Better quality
land was shared out in strips and the grazing on poorer
pasture was communal. The grazings higher up on the
hills were also held in common and in summer the
young people of the clachan would move up to the high
pastures to live in the little huts called sheilings. The
main livestock were cattle, the small, black, sturdy
beasts found all over the Highlands. Ponies were kept
for farm work and transport and the principal crops
were oats and barley, with perhaps a small kailyard for
vegetables. This subsistence economy depended also
on fishing and Loch Fyne herrings were a substantial
export both to the South and to the Continent.

Another important export in the Highlands were the
black cattle which were driven "on the hoof" to the great
markets at Crieff, Falkirk and Carlisle. In his exhaustive
study "The Drove Roads of Scotland" A R Haldane
describes the routes by which the animals were driven
to these markets. Many of the routes from the West
and North converged in Cowal. Cattle were brought,
for example, from Mid-Argyll and Kintyre up to the
south end of Loch Awe, from where they were driven

over the track across the hills to Loch Fyne. This track is now signposted as a Public Footpath. They were ferried across the loch and then driven over the hill to Ardentinny or brought down the west side of Loch Eck to Dunoon to be ferried across the Clyde. Part of the old drove road can still be seen near Loch Loskin.

Argyll did not suffer as much as other parts of the Highlands from the infamous "Clearances" when landowners evicted their tenants by force to make way for large sheep farms. The use of the land did, however change. About 1750 a mysterious stranger, Thomas Harkness, known as "an Gall Ruadh", (the red-haired stranger) appeared in Cowal driving 15 sheep before him. He acquired the farm of Glenkin and became extremely prosperous. He died at the age of 91, having had fourteen children, the youngest born when he was 82.

Another interesting development was the use of timber. Oakwoods were coppiced on a twenty year rotation to give poles and firewood. The bark was also used in tanning leather. Charcoal was another valuable product and was essential for smelting bog-iron which was reasonably plentiful. This technique had changed very little over the centuries.

A new industrial development was the setting up of gunpowder factories at Millhouse, near Kames, and in Glenlean near Dunoon. The ruins of the houses and of the gunpowder stores - widely separated, for obvious reasons - can still be seen. Barrels to contain the gunpowder from Glenlean were made at the Cooperage in Sandbank, now the site of a filling station, and then taken to ships lying at the Tail of the Bank.

In spite of this there was little prosperity in the villages along the coast of Cowal. In 1823 "The Scottish Tourist's Companion" stated of Dunoon, "The village is in a state of decay". Yet in 1857, only thirty-four years later MacDonald's "Days at the Coast" says, "No other section of our coast, indeed, has been so densely peopled as that in the vicinity of Dunoon", and adds, "It has become the splendid assemblage of mingled mansions and cottages, villas and gardens which .... now gladdens the eye". MacDonald himself gives the explanation when he writes, "Modern Dunoon has been called into existence by the genius of steam". The first sailing of the "Comet" in 1812 marked the beginning of a new era.

Cowal, which had been regarded as a remote, Gaelic-speaking, crofting area, developed closer links with the other side of the Firth and particularly with the fast-growing city of Glasgow up the River Clyde. As George Blake says in "Cruise in Company", the history of the Royal Clyde Yacht Club, "It was the steamboat that stirred these hamlets into life". Soon there was a great increase in regular steamer services. It became practicable to travel to Glasgow to one's place of business while living in an unspoiled district of great scenic beauty.

This development had begun in Dunoon in 1822 when Lord Provost James Ewing of Glasgow bought the grounds of the Castle and built a fine summer residence. He called it "Castle House" and it still stands within its gardens over-looking the Pier. Until the reorganisation of local government in 1974 it housed the Council Chambers and the Provost's Room, and it still contains the Tulloch Library. It is said that local cottages were demolished to provide space for the

Castle House, Dunoon

mansion and Ewing soon provoked local hostility when he used the stones from the ancient Castle to build a wall around his new home. As the wall was built by his masons by day, so it was demolished by the local women by night. The land round the Castle had always been regarded as common property and was much used for bleaching linen. Eventually the women were arrested and taken to Inveraray for trial. However, they were only bound over to be of good behaviour, and Ewing compromised by leaving them the slopes of the Castle Hill.

Many other wealthy Glasgow businessmen and industrialists built fine mansions as summer residences. It must have been a complicated operation to transfer an entire household, with children and servants, to the coast for four months every year.

Their example was copied by many more and a thriving holiday trade grew up. Roads were improved, piers were built and hotels were established to provide accommodation for those not in the social position of having their own summer homes. The seaside landlady made her appearance and the golden age of "Doon the Watter" had begun.

Many of the wealthier residents in the Clyde holiday resorts enjoyed sailing in what are arguably the finest cruising waters in Britain. They wished to have their own yachts and a number of yards sprang up on the shores of the Firth to satisfy this demand. Among these were two of the best-known, Robertson's and Morris & Lorimer's at Sandbank. Hunter's Quay was an important centre of yacht racing and the headquarters of the Royal Clyde Yacht Club were at the Royal Marine Hotel there. "Sceptre", "Sovereign" and Kurrewa",.three challengers for the famous America's Cup were all built at Sandbank. Changing social conditions during the post-war years led to the decline of Hunter's Quay as a yachting centre, while the advent of factory production of glass reinforced plastic yachts led to the demise of the yards in the 80s.

Clyde Steamers

In 1812 the "Comet" had changed travel on the Clyde for ever. No longer was water travel dependent on

One of Dunoon's 19th century landmarks.

wind and tide, and steam propulsion made rapid
progress during the next two decades.

During 1830-1840 the Napier family were important in
the development of steamers. David Napier is
particularly associated, too, with the development of
Kilmun, where he had his home. In 1829 he began
building the village - houses, a pier and a hotel. He
introduced the first steamboat on Loch Eck and ran a
steam carriage between Kilmun and Inverchapel on
Loch Eck to connect with the steamer. This was the
fore-runner of the famous Loch Eck Tour.

By the 1840s iron had superseded wood in the building
of steamers. This led to an increase in their size and a
corresponding increase in comfort. These paddle
steamers were owned by private individuals - David
Napier, P & A Campbell of Kilmun, Gillies, MacKellar,
Williamson, Buchanan and MacBrayne. The continued
improvement of the steam engine led to increasing
speeds, with the various builders vying with each other
to produce the fastest vessel. There was little
improvement in the standard of comfort except in a few
isolated cases.

The outbreak of the American Civil War in 1861 and the
blockade imposed by the North on the Southern States
led to a demand for fast, shallow-draught vessels to
beat the blockade. The best of the Clyde fleet were
sold to the Confederates. Only the oldest and slowest
vessels remained in the Clyde. As a result there was
an upsurge in building new ships, which were designed
for passenger comfort. During that decade no fewer
than 43 paddle steamers were built for private owners.
Deck saloons were introduced and more luxurious
accommodation. This trend culminated in the

Tighnabruaich Pier

magnificent "Columba" of 1875.

In the latter quarter of the century the principal railway companies built up their own fleets of steamers. These companies were Caledonian Steam Packet Company, Glasgow & South Western Railway Company, and North British Railway Company. The standards of both comfort and performance were improved. To this period belong some of the most famous of Clyde steamers - "Duchess of Hamilton" (I), "Caledonia" (I), "Mercury" (I), "Jupiter" (I), "Glen Sannox" (I), "Jeanie Deans" (I), "Kenilworth" and "Lucy Ashton".

This steady improvement continued up to and through the First World War, culminating in such favourites as the "Duchess of Montrose" II, "Duchess of Hamilton" II and "Queen Mary".

After the Second World War the rapid and dramatic increase in the popularity of the motor car resulted in the decline of Clyde cruising and the introduction and development of the car ferry. The only traditional Clyde steamer left, the "Waverley", still cruises on the Clyde and round the coasts of the British Isles, maintaining

The old Waverley calling at Kirn Pier - drawn from a 1901 photograph

the proud tradition of the Clyde steamers.

Wars and Threats of War

During the two World Wars the Clyde was of great
importance. In both wars an anti-submarine boom was
stretched across the Firth from Dunoon to the Cloch
Lighthouse. It consisted of a steel net suspended from
floating buoys and reaching to the sea bed. There was
a "gate" which could be opened to allow the passage of
shipping. Behind this protection the sheltered
anchorage was packed with ships which had brought
supplies of food and war material to the great docks of
the Clyde.

In World War II Sandbank on the Holy Loch was a submarine base, the best known submarine depot ship being H M S Forth. It was also a base for fast armed motor launches. The two yacht-building yards at Sandbank were engaged in the construction of small specialised craft for the Royal Navy and the Royal Air Force. H M S Osprey was actually a shore establishment used as a submarine officers' training base and was in the Convalescent Homes, Argyll Street, Dunoon. The building has since been demolished. Many local hotels became naval quarters for the duration of the war.

Loch Fyne and its shores were used as Commando training areas, and a museum relating to this has been set up in Inveraray, which was their headquarters.

Submarines returned to the Holy Loch in 1961 when the United States Navy nuclear submarine base was established there. There was considerable opposition to the siting of a potentially dangerous base so near large centres of population and the arrival of the first depot ship, the "Proteus" was greeted by protesting demonstrators ashore and also afloat on the Holy Loch in small boats. As time passed, the American presence became accepted. Many local girls married U S sailors and went to the States; some U S personnel liked the area so well that on the completion of their service they "went native" and settled down here. Although the U S Navy had their own sport and entertainment complexes, as well as a PX store stocking American goods, and their own filling station selling "gas", their children were educated in local schools and this provided a link with the local community. A succession of depot ships lay in the Holy Loch for 31 years, while their submarines with their deadly missiles slipped in and out of the Firth - part of the American defences in the "cold war". A visible sign of the "peace dividend" was the departure of the floating dock and the last depot ship in the Spring of 1992.

About 1974 there was a short-lived flurry of industrial activity when a yard to build oil rigs was established at Ardyne, near Toward. A number of giant rigs were floated out into the Firth. A second yard was planned at the equally beautiful Portavadie on Loch Fyneside. It never became operational and all that is left of a once beautiful bay is a giant hole and a ghost village. The Ardyne operation closed after several years and part of the site is now used as a fish farm. In spite of promises given at the time neither site has been restored to its former condition.

It is difficult to imagine what will be the next development in Cowal's long history. The past has been moulded by its geographical location and its easy access by sea and loch, which has brought settlers from Mesolithic shell-gatherers to American submariners. Who will be next?

Dunoon & Cowal Now

Access into the Cowal peninsula is confined principally to two routes, one land and the other by sea. The land route is by the A83 road from Glasgow and Loch Lomondside, turning onto the A8l5 in Glen Kinglas, about 28 miles from Dunoon. Most people come to Cowal via Dunoon using the two ferry routes. Caledonian MacBrayne operate an hourly car and passenger service from the railhead at Gourock Pier to Dunoon Pier. Western Ferries operate a car and passenger service at half-hourly (or less) interval from MacInroy's Point, some two miles west of Gourock to Hunter's Quay. Both journeys take 20-25 minutes. During summer months the Waverley and Keppel run cruises to other Clyde resorts, notably Largs, Rothesay and Campbeltown. The Caledonian MacBrayne ferry at Colintraive operates a frequent car and passenger service between Cowal and North Bute.

Cowal and Dunoon are well provided with a range of hotels, guest houses, bed and breakfast and self-catering accommodation. Details can be found in the Dunoon and Cowal Tourist Board's brochure. Numerically there are about 50 hotel and guest houses in Cowal (about 35 in Dunoon), with a further 30 bed and breakfast establishments and over 40 self-catering houses, lodges and chalets.

Climate

The best times to visit Dunoon and Cowal are late-Spring, early Summer or the early Autumn. May, June and September probably have the most reliable weather when it is quite sunny, warm and dry. However inevitable climatic variations can produce remarkably dry and sunny days in January and wet, cold ones in June! July and August, peak tourist months, can be hot and dry, but equally wet and cool. The area has few frost or snowy days being so close to ameliorating Atlantic currents and winds; wind directions are often south-west or westerly. In general South Cowal around Innellan and Toward is drier than North Cowal, where hills are higher and more concentrated.

Cowal: Population and Economy

Dunoon is by far the largest town in Argyll, the former County town, before Regionalisation granted that honour to Lochgilphead as the new District headquarters. Dunoon's resident population is approximately 13,000, out of a total population for Cowal of 17,000. The size of Dunoon is best appreciated from the Clyde - there is almost continuous built-up coastal area from Blairmore to Toward, linking what were originally quite separate communities, each with their own pier. Compared to this coastal development the rest of Cowal is sparsely peopled, particularly in the west and north apart from centres like

Strachur, Lochgoilhead and Tighnabruaich.

In terms of employment Dunoon and Cowal have become a "fragile" economy, too reliant on the continued presence of the American Navy to bolster an otherwise weak manufacturing or tourist base. Up to the 1950s Dunoon especially relied heavily on "doon the watter" visitors. These have been replaced by more discerning tourists who are fewer in number.

Over three quarters of employed people in Cowal work in the "service" sector, the largest employer being Dunoon General Hospital, though local authority employees (Strathclyde Region and Argyll and Bute District) have a very strong contingent as workers in education; housing; social work; police; fire; libraries; roads and environmental health. Forestry and agriculture are major employers - about a third of Cowal has commercial forests - and farming of sheep, dairy and fish - is widespread throughout Cowal. The construction industry is locally important and other private sector industries include Dunoon Pottery, one of the largest. The area's hotel and bed and breakfast establishments are also important employers particularly of part-time and seasonal workers, a key "industry" which will be in the forefront of the regeneration of Cowal.

Unemployment is fickle, rising and falling with the seasonal change as tourists come and go. Even so there is a difficult underlying stubbornness to reduce the figures with real jobs, particularly now that one of Cowal's major economic props has departed. Unemployment figures are higher than the national Scottish average and will remain so until regeneration provides expanded and diversified employment opportunities for local people.

Education

The scattered rural population of much of Cowal favours small primary schools. These are located at Ardentinny, Strone, Sandbank, Rashfield, Strachur, Lochgoilhead, Tighnabruaich, Glendaruel, Toward and Innellan. Dunoon has three primary schools, the largest at Kirn with over 300 pupils. The secondary school for Cowal is Dunoon Grammar School, a large comprehensive school up to 6th Form level, with a roll of over 900 pupils and 75 staff. There is no college in the area, the nearest is James Watt Further Education College at Greenock. The nearest universities are in Glasgow. An important Careers and Community Education service operates in Cowal and agencies such as the WEA and Glasgow University provide a range of adult education courses. Two Outdoor Centres (Benmore and Ardentinny) provide field and outdoor courses for schools mainly outwith Argyll.

Leisure Facilities

In this short section only the briefest information is provided, more can be obtained from Dunoon and Cowal Tourist Information Centre or from Dunoon Library.

There are two main centres where leisure facilities are concentrated - Gateway Leisure in Dunoon which has a Swimming Pool, Sauna, Health and Fitness Suite and organise various activities. Drymsynie Leisure Centre at Lochgoilhead operates a wide range of leisure facilities - swimming pool, indoor bowling, ice skating, golf course and pony trekking. For golfers there are excellent golf courses in Cowal - Cowal Golf Course, Ardenslate, Dunoon; Innellan; Blairmore; and Kyles of Bute. Five bowling greens can be found in the Dunoon/Sandbank area with another at Ardentinny. Tennis courts are situated at Castle Gardens and Innellan. Sailing is concentrated at Toward and Holy Loch, where there are clubs, with a specialist Sailing School at Tighnabruaich offering dingy sailing courses and windsurfing in the Kyles of Bute. Other water sports - such as diving and water skiing - can be pursued at Loch Goil and the Kyles of Bute. Innellan has an excellent pony trekking centre at Velvet Path. Cowal attracts many fishermen to its lochs, rivers and water bodies. For the walker the hills of Cowal provide endless delights and a series of Forest Walks and trails have been published by the local Tourist Centre in conjunction with the Forestry Commission.

Dunoon's Library is situated at Castle House, but moves to a new site on Argyll Street in 1993. Three new facilities now grace Dunoon - Dunoon and Cowal Heritage Centre has an excellent display of many of the area's historical and cultural traditions, particularly Clyde Steamers. The second is the audio-visual "Argyll Experience" and the third is the Clan Centre, all at the Argyll Hotel, Dunoon.

Dunoon and Cowal's Future

With the withdrawal of the American Holy Loch Naval Base in 1992 Dunoon and Cowal is faced with a period of economic and social re-adjustment which is a new and daunting prospect. At a stroke the area has lost a quarter of its population (there were over 4,000 personnel and families at the Base), a substantial employer and provider of revenue. There will be considerable knock-on effects throughout the local communities - amongst the retailers, businesses, schools and housing. It has been estimated that Base closure will cost Cowal £10 million in lost income and several hundred jobs.

In response to threatened economic dislocation local and central government agencies, together with the European Community, are prepared to fund a regeneration of Cowal amounting to many millions of pounds. The newly formed Argyll and the Isles Enterprise Company established a Steering Group to co-ordinate the initiative and prepare an Action Plan. The ambitious Plan envisages "the retention and creation of at least 900 jobs by 1996", the main thrust being to improve and extend the tourist base for Dunoon and Cowal involving job creation, business establishment and a need to upgrade roads and ferries. The total regeneration package could cost £40 million, but only a fraction of that has been forthcoming so far.

Whatever way government or agency funds are directed the people who live in Dunoon and Cowal must be consulted at every stage to avoid arbitrary or imposed projects which may not be long-lived or productive. Cowal deserves the best promotion at all levels to attract more people to visit the area year after year as they used to do. Equally there is no merit in attracting visitors if they are so disappointed by what they find or experience that they do not return.

Ironically Cowal has so much to offer in terms of scenery, environment, leisure opportunities and the very high quality of life in the peninsula, yet has remained a relatively remote and hidden part of the Scottish Highlands. Improved access is one way of attracting more people to holiday here - cheaper ferry fares would help both locals and visitors alike and better information facilities at the crucial "entry points" into Cowal such as at the rather bleak Glen Kinglas road turn and at ferry piers. Couple this with improvements within Cowal - regeneration - to improve standards and image then increasing number of visitors will want to return and provide the economy with a reliable base for the future.

Gazetteer

Ardnadam

Adam's Grave (NS 162 800) Neolithic burial cairn is visible on the left from the Dunoon-Sandbank High Road just before the road drops down into Sandbank. The cairn has been removed but the stones of the chamber with its large capstone are impressive.

Ardnadam Chapel (NS 163 791) The tradition that a chapel and a burial ground lay here led to its excavation by Cowal Archaeological Society over a number of years. The chapel, which has a stone altar, and a preaching knoll nearby is visible, though stones with a cross, which may have been grave markers, are now in the Hunterian Museum, Glasgow.

Ardno, Loch Fyne

(NN 156 080) Bronze Age round cairn in the area to the south of the junction of the Hell's Glen road to Lochgoilhead and the main road (A886). This cairn shows the cist, although the capstone has disappeared.

Ardyne

Parking is plentiful near Toward Quay. The rocks around the Sailing Club have Rock Pipits, and the sandy beach may have Ringed Plovers, with Eider and Mergansers on the water. The field may hold Redshank, Lapwing,

Oystercatchers and Snipe, and in winter a flock of Greylags that overspill from Bute. The trees in the grounds of Toward Castle Residential Centre have a heronry. The outflow of the Ardyne burn often attracts a pair of Mute Swans, and Shelduck, with Dippers and Wagtails on the burn itself. In recent years a number of Whimbrel have been regular passage visitors in May.

Ardyne Point was developed during the 1970s as a building site for offshore platforms for the North Sea Oil Industry. Two deep pits were dug into raised beach deposits exposing stratified clays and sands with fossil shells. The shells enabled geologists to date the layers to 12000 years ago when sea levels were higher than today and a colder water fauna lived around the shores.

Argyll Forest Park

This first Forest Park was established in 1935 by the Forestry Commission and occupies 150 square miles, most of it in Cowal. The Park offers substantial animal and bird life, opportunities for walking and cycling well off the beaten track with fishing in lochs and rivers.

Kilmun Arboretum overlooks Holy Loch extending some 180 acres with a wide range of forest and ornamental tree species. There are three well marked trails lasting half hour to one-and-a-half hours.

Bishop's Glen

On the outskirts of west Dunoon, this is a popular walk with folk from the town. Parking is possible in Auchamore Road and Kilbride Road. The centrepiece is the former drinking water reservoir which is now a fishing lochan and is stocked with Rainbow Trout by Dunoon and District Angling Club. The immediate surrounds are in the care of the District Council who look upon it as an unofficial country park. The surrounding commercial forests to the south are Forestry Commission and to the north Tilhill Economic Forestry. The walk up from the town from Auchamore Road goes up through mixed woodland to the lochan with a deep gorge to the left. The lochan itself may have Dippers, Common

Sandpiper, Wagtails, a Little Grebe, Mallard, Grey Heron or Goldeneye. Besides the usual woodland species (including Redstart, Tree Pipit, Wood Warbler) the clearfell area to the south may have Whitethroat, Grasshopper Warbler, Stonechat and Cuckoo.

Blairmore-Gairletter-Glen Finart

From Kilmun to Blairmore the shore road follows the post-glacial raised beach with abandoned cliffs. Around Blairmore Farm and Gairletter increasing sand and gravel outcrops mark the major ice terminus 10,000 years ago, the meltwater point for Lomond Ice, with occurrences of bedded sands, kames, terraces and meltwater channels. Between Blairmore and Stronchullin Burns attempts were made in the 19th Century to mine silver. James Duncan (a former owner of Benmore) opened up trial levels into faulted schist rock, one 250 m long, to recover silver, but the venture produced only a little argentiferous lead and was abandoned. Glen Finart is another glacially-cut valley terminating in a raised beach sequence below Glen Finart House. The shore near the outlet of the Finart Burn reveals good outcrops of contorted schist and schistose grit. Further up the glen are good ice erosional features - striations and glacially plucked bedrock (Larach Hill).

From Strone point to Ardentinny the road follows the rocky beach, enabling the birdwatcher the luxury of using the car as a hide. The single track road is surprisingly busy with traffic including tour buses and timber trucks, so thoughtfulness is needed when stopping to view. Shags and Cormorants both roost on the Admiralty mooring Buoys at Blairmore. At the mouth of the Blairmore Burn the outwash fan provides a roosting site for gulls and waders close to the road. Eider and Merganser occur inshore, with Oystercatchers, Curlew and Redshank feeding at the water's edge. At high tide the waders can often be seen probing the soil in the fields of pasture. Crows are a common sight, flying into the air with mussels before dropping them onto the rocks to break the shells. The mud and shingle in Finart Bay at Ardentinny is another area where birds concentrate and is worth a look.

Carrick Castle, Loch Goil
(NS 193 945) A handsome tower of 14th century construction in a commanding position on the west shore of Loch Goil. Mary Queen of Scots is said to have spent a night in this castle during her visit to Argyyll in 1563.

Castle Lachlan
(NS 005 952) This ruined castle is in a commanding position on Loch Fyne. It is probably 15th century and was occupied until the late 18th century.

Colintraive
(NS 032 744) Near the ferry terminal at Colintraive and set in a field is a large Bronze Age round cairn.

Cowal Highland Gathering
One of the main Cowal attractions at the end of August every year is the Highland Gathering. Now over a century since the first Games, the event is a crowd-puller with over 100 bands competing in the Pipe Band Contest and the celebrated March Past.

Dunan Hill
Dunan Hill is the prominent ridge overlooking the town from the north. The ridge continues into Ardenslate forming a high feature on Cowal Golf Course and represents the outcrop of a particularly hard rock (hornblende schist) once quarried for road stone hereabouts. The ridge has quite spectacular ice scratches, showing two ice movements - north-south and northwest-southeast. Loch Loskin sits in a deep cleft caused by ice erosion. The lochan is ponded back by an obvious glacial moraine.

Dunoon Castle
This was a Royal Castle and the keeper was the head of the Campbell clan. The nominal rent was a red rose to be presented whenever the sovereign visited the castle and this was done in 1958 when the present Queen visited Dunoon. Little remains of the original castle and the commanding site

was used as an emplacement for guns and searchlights during both World Wars. Much of the stone had been removed in 1822 when James Ewing purchased the site to build the Castle House.

Dunoon Castle Hill

Castle Hill is an excellent vantage point for views down and across the Clyde estuary. The Clyde masks the course of the Highland Boundary Fault between Innellan Pier and Kilcreggan, where there is a clear notch in the skyline marking the line of the fault. The hills behind the Cloch and Gourock are made of 340 million year old lava flows, the terraced flows standing out as "trap" topography. Ailsa Craig is the pipe which 60 million years ago fed a substantial volcano, the pipe is filled with a microgranite, once quarried for curling stones. Castle Hill, Highland Mary and the Rock Cafe all stand on a 290 million year old intruded dyke, about 30 m wide and vertically cut into the local Dunoon Phyllites, well exposed in Castle Gardens. The contact of the dyke rock (dolerite) and phyllite is visible on the shore by the café.

Dunoon High Kirk

is probably on the site of a chapel connected with the castle. The present church dates from the re-building of the old in 1816. The Bishops of Argyll had a palace, now on the site of the school playground.

Glen Finart Deer Farm

Glen Finart Deer Farm is situated at Barnacabber Farm, near Ardentinny. The Visitor Centre provides deer tours and videos of deer farming and local wildlife.

Glen Lean

Glen Lean is a fine example of a glacially eroded "U"-shaped valley, ice moving towards Holy Loch. Between Clachaig and Corrachaive are *roches moutonnees* - glacially eroded bedrock which formed a barrier to moving ice and was consequently plucked and polished. The feature bears ice striations. Nearby the entrance to Corrachaive has a superb terminal moraine, a ridge of ice pushed boulders and gravel making the limit of ice advance from the corrie 11,000 years ago. At Ballochyle are glacial meltwater features - kames and sand ridges which represent tunnel infilling at the foot of a melting ice tongue, perhaps 14,000 years old.

Glen Massan

Glen Massan is a superb glacially eroded valley with good ice scratches, the best being at the roadside a little north of the Golden Gates. Further up the glen is another important site, a group of waterfalls cut into hard schistose grit bedrocks. This is a knick point, the site where the river is cutting into its bed adjusting to fallen sea levels in the Clyde. Above the falls the river flows in a sequence of meanders across the flat floor of the old glacial valley.

Glenan Forest Nature Reserve, Portavadie

It is a long drive round hill and loch from Dunoon to Glenan, but on a fine summer's day, well worth the trouble. Rewarding views across Loch Fyne to distant Tarbet give a feeling of remoteness. The drive over the moorland from Millhouse gives views across to Arran, and the chance of Cuckoos and even Hen Harrier. The footpath leads from the picnic site through the oakwood by the shore, then splits, with one path following the shore round to Glenan Bay, and the other striking over the hill to reunite with the Shore, also in Glenan Bay. Oystercatchers and Ringed Plover nest on the beach in well camouflaged scrapes, so place your feet with care. On offshore islands, Black Guillemot and gulls breed. Mergansers, Eider and Cormorants fish the shallows, and Shags fish the deeper rocky waters. Gannets from Ailsa Craig are frequently seen. The spring time woods vibrate with the calls and song of tits and warblers, while the Buzzard mews overhead.

Glenbranter Forest Walks

A car park with forest walks are situated close to the forestry village. The deciduous and coniferous woodland, and pastures offer a sheltered walk in windy weather, especially if it is from the north west. The usual woodland, river and farmland species can be found, plus the chance of Pied Flycatchers, and the fleeting glimpse of Peregrine flashing by. Eagles too might be sighted high on the hill. In fine weather at dusk and dawn in the spring, the warbling of Blackcock can carry over some distance.

Glendaruel

Glendaruel is one of the largest and longest glaciated valleys in Cowal, its lower course now drowned by Loch Riddon. The glen has important meltwater features at Dun an Oir and in neighbouring Strath nan Lub, which have enabled geologists to date the last ice advance to 11,000 years ago. The glen has outcrops of Loch Tay limestone in the slopes above the West Road and "green beds" exposed near the Clachan. Copper ores were found in the schists here in the 19th Century near the Clachan and a recent appraisal of their meagre metal content found insufficient copper to warrant economic extraction.

The striking red soils of the Glen originated from Ice Age weathering of local rock (the red colour is a typical weathering concentration of iron oxide) eventually laid down by the River Ruel in the flat-floored Glen.

Holy Loch

The estuary at the west shore of the Holy Loch holds the greatest concentrations of birds found anywhere in Cowal. The extensive mudflats provide a large feeding area for waders and wildfowl when the tide is out and at high tide the neighbouring pastures and saltmarshes provide an alternative foraging and roosting area. The nearby rubbish tip (now trendily known by the euphemism landfill site) at Dalinlongart is highly attractive to gulls, who commute from the estuary when tipping is in progress. The observation point on the Sandbank shore from Broxwood car park, has the advantage of the light behind the observer but a more distant view. From the Kilmun shore near the forest office the views are closer, but into the light except before mid-morning.

Holy Loch Farm Park

Holy Loch Farm Park is a working farm with a substantial range of animals - Highland Cattle; Clydesdale Horses; Pot-bellied Pigs and many varieties of Sheep - Soay; Welsh Mountain; Jacob and Loghtan. Plus many rare poultry breeds. Situated one mile north of Sandbank at the road turn to Colintraive.

Innellan

Knockamillie Castle (NS 152 710) The striking fragment of this castle stands above Innellan. It probably dates from the mid-16th century.

Inverglen, Strachur

(NN 097 018) This Iron Age site is close to the road leading from Strachur to Inverglen Farm. The surrounding wall can still be traced.

Kames Gunpowder Miill

From 1839 to 1921 gunpowder was manufactured at Millhouse, raw materials being imported via Kames Pier. A number of buildings are still visible, notably the Gatehouse and Mill Magazine.

Kilfinan Church

(NR 934 788) There has been a church here since the 13th century. The present church dates from the middle of the 18th century. It was restored in the 1880's. The Lamont Vault, with interesting stones, is entered from the churchyard and is well worth a visit.

Kilfinan

Ach-na-ha Neolithic Cairn. (NR 933 819) Hidden in forestry planting - 1 mile south of the junction of Otter Ferry - Glendaruel roads. The burial chambers and the forecourt are still to be seen, but the cairn covering it was removed centuries ago.

Kyles of Bute from viewpoint

Kilmodan Church, Glendaruel

(NR 995 841) This attractivce building dates from 1783.
Internally it has an interesting layout with three Lairds
Galleries - for the Campbells of Glendaruel, the Campbells of
South Hall, and the Campbells of Ormidale.

Kilmorich, Cairndow

(NN 180 107) An unusual octagonal church of 1816, which
contains a medieval fort.

Kilmun

(NS 166 820) An important early Christian site. The parish
church was a collegiate church attached to Paisley Abbey

and is recorded as such in 1442.
Dr Elizabeth Blackwell, the first woman doctor to be
registered in Britain, is buried in the graveyard. Kilmun is also
the burial place of the Dukes of Argyll; their mausoleum
dates from 1794.

Kyles of Bute

Viewpoints above the Kyles of Bute along the road to
Tighnabruaich provide some of Scotland's most magnificent
scenery, with evidence of deep glacial erosion in every view.
The Burnt Islands are remains of the old land bridge to Bute,
with good raised beach features along both East and West
Kyles and at the head of Loch Riddon. The Arran Mountains

around Goat Fell are well seen from this road. Arran is a 60 million year old volcanic centre, the northern mountains being built from a massive granite intrusion.

The East Kyle is the most accessible by car, from the Colintraive shore and the Bute shore, although the light is better from the Bute side. The Eider, Shag and Mergansers are joined in winter by Goldeneye and Little Grebes. The Burnt Islands are home to breeding Herring and Great Black Back Gulls, and a favourite haunt of Common Seals.

Loch Eck

An area popular with freshwater anglers, especially in spring before the midges emerge, and increasingly with speedboats and water skiers. This shouldn't be a put-off, since it is 7 miles long and most activity is centred around the Coylet Inn. There are many laybys and picnic sites beside the public main road on the east shore. The forest road on the west shore has several locked gates, but makes a very pleasant walk or cycle compared to the busy main road. Goosanders are the star water bird on the loch, although present only in small numbers. Mallard, Dippers, Wagtails and Common Sandpipers can be seen almost anywhere along the shore. The only island, by Dornoch Bay, is a popular roost for Cormorants, as is the outflow from the River Cur at the north end. This spot is an interesting area of fen and carr, rich in invertebrates, with Reed Bunting and Sedge Warblers.

The coniferous and deciduous woods around the loch can be explored on foot by the network of forest roads. A recent colonist is the Pied Flycatcher. Above the forest the mountain tops are worth a scan with binoculars for eagles, buzzards and ravens.

Stratheck and Loch Eck lie in a large glaciated valley, possibly fault controlled. Around Coylet are excellent road exposures of grey quartz-mica schist, with intense crumpling and folding quite obvious. To the west of the loch are examples of hanging valleys (Bernice Glen) where tributary glaciers once flowed out to join the main ice in the Eck valley. Puck's Glen has a magnificent display of waterfalls running over silvery mica-schists. Although Loch Eck is comparatively shallow it was once joined via Holy Loch to the Clyde 14,000 years ago. The presence of the powan, a freshwater herring, testifies to the old sea connection.

Loch Goil

Loch Goil is another drowned glacial valley, cut north-south against the prevailing rock strike. An underwater rock barrier shallows the entrance to the loch to a mere l4m, though the inner part of the loch drops to 86 m.

Carrick Castle stands on glaciated schist, the hard quartz-mica schists are smoothed and scratched by ice along the shore. Glen Mor leads up to Rest-and-Be-Thankful in a long glacial valley, cut to a lower level than Hell's Glen, which hangs above the main Glen. Hell's Glen has a notable landslip of recent origin, which narrows the valley.

Lochgoilhead

(NS 198 014)   Church of the Three Holy Brethren. It appears that there has been a church on this site since early Christian times, possibly 7th century. The origin of the name is unknown. The church is mainly 15th century work with later additions.

Lochgoilhead European Sheep and Wool Centre

The European Sheep and Wool Centre is situated at Lochgoilhead with displays of 19 different breeds of sheep and sheep shearing demonstrations.

Loch Riddon

A huge area of sand and mud are exposed when the tide is out. It is best viewed from the west side, where the road to Tighnabruaich hugs the shore. Mute Swans, Mallard and Shelduck are regular breeders, and Oystercatchers, Redshank and Lapwing often feed and roost there. Eider and Common Sandpiper breed all round the shore, and a colony of Common Gulls nest near the junction with the Kyles of Bute. On the River Ruel a colony of Sand Martins sometimes occupies a large river cliff on the last big meander before the sea, although erosion is a problem for them.

Otter Ferry

The presence of limestone in West Cowal is testified by old lime kilns and quarries along the strike of the rock The limestone was burnt for agricultural lime. Otter Ferry is famous for its substantial shingle spit (*Oitir*) built up by sea currents in Loch Fyne on a submerged rock barrier or glacial moraine.

The high road over to Glendaruel rises to over 300 m giving panoramic views over Loch Fyne and Loch Gilp as far as the Paps of Jura and Mull.

Barr Iola (NR 938 828) A very well preserved Iron Age *dun* with a magnificent view. The defensive wall is still standing to a considerable extent.

Rest-and-be-Thankful Glen Croe

The Rest-and-Be-Thankful provides a superb viewpoint for the highest scenery in Cowal with views of Ben Arthur and Ben Ime. Glen Croe is an outstanding glacial valley, cut by successive waves of erosion, the last time only 11,000 years ago. Loch Restil is ponded back by glacial debris in a rock basin eroded by ice from upper Glen Kinglas moving south into Glen Croe and Glen Mor. Glen Kinglas is a hanging valley, ice in Glen Fyne eroded to a greater depth leaving tributary valleys, such as Glen Kinglas, "hanging".

Lower Glen Croe has excellent erosional features, ice plucked and polished surfaces particularly clear where the glen narrows into the gorge above Creagdhu. The Croe Water drains into Loch Long at Ardgarten where it forms a large delta, indicating its post-glacial origin. Loch Long is deeply incised into the hard schist rocks as a drowned glacially-cut valley along a northeast to southwest alignment. The pass over the Rest and Be Thankful is a central point from which to explore the higher hills of Cowal. However the weather and visibility here can be quite severe and changeable, and the terrain treacherous, so inexperienced hillwalkers would do well not to stray too far from the road. Unlike much of Cowal the hills here are less clothed with conifer forest, and remain sheepwalk. Trees are confined by the grazing of sheep to inaccessible slopes. Nevertheless, Wrens can be heard surprisingly high up. Meadow Pipits abound, and the rockier corries sometimes ring to the song of Ring Ouzels and Wheatears, with Ravens croaking overhead. Buzzards soar high, searching for rabbits and mountain hares, fooling many that they are eagles, which also occur.

Strachur-St Catherines

The Loch Tay limestone makes a small outcrop in Glen Sluan, where it was formerly quarried for both agricultural lime and road metal last century. At Strachur are excellent views down Loch Fyne, deep water here goes down 140 m into a glacially eroded trough, cut in weaker phyllites. On the opposite shore are large microgranite outcrops, quarried at Furnace and formerly at Crarae for building stone and road metal. Much of Inveraray is built from this attractive pink stone. Sithean Sluaigh (435 m) a little south of Strachur is the conical pipe which fed a 60 million year old volcano, the pipe infilled with dolerite. The hill is best viewed from the Creggans shore or from the opposite side of Loch Fyne. The schists around Strachur are noted for brown-red garnets, best found in beach pebbles near Creggans.

At St Catherines are former quarries which supplied stone for the 18th Century re-build of Inveraray Castle. Fifty stonemasons were employed in the quarries to cut and dress stone, an attractive green chlorite schist. Other rock was once quarried for road metal, notably dykes of dolerite and felsite which occur hereabouts.

The road north from St Catherines reveals unsurpassed views to the head of Loch Fyne, which exhibits all the signs of a superb glacial valley leading into Glen Fyne.

Strachur Church (NN 095 015) The churchyard which is circular, is typical of an Early Christian site. The present church is 18th century

Toward Castle

(NS 118 678) The ruined tower of this Lamont castle is visible from the road just after passing Toward village. There is a very fine arched gateway. The tower is the oldest part of the castle and probably dated from the 15th century, while the hall area with its three apartments is more likely to be from the middle of the 16th century.

Toward Shore

The shore at Toward Point, near the Lighthouse, exposes Old Red Sandstone and limestone with intruded dykes The best one appears at the end of the shore wall where a fault displaces the course of the dyke. There are large glacial erratics hereabouts, including a boulder of Glen Fyne granite, dropped by ice 20,000 years ago.

West of Toward School are more dykes and good sandstone outcrops as far as the upstanding edges of the Highland Boundary Fault, opposite Toward Castle. Note how the sandstone is wrapped around the fault breccia (angular broken rock) with serpentine within the fault zone and a large Tertiary dyke cut into the actual fault.

The fault runs inland past Toward Farm, near where talc was quarried in the 1920s for ornamental stone. Offshore the fault runs into Rothesay Bay. There are fine views to Canada Hill, Bute (Old Red Sandstone), Ascog Hill (lavas) and to Little Cumbrae where six individual lava flows stand out clearly.

Younger Botanic Gardens, Benmore

The Younger Botanic Gardens, Benmore, has become world-renowned for its collection of shrubs and trees, especially Rhododendron (250 species), Azalea and giant Californian Redwoods forming a superb avenue of tall trees. The Gardens are an outstation of Edinburgh's Royal Botanic Gardens and were first planted in the 1870s by James Duncan. The Younger family continued the development from 1883 to 1928, when the estate was gifted to the nation. Situated seven miles north of Dunoon on the A815 Glasgow road, the gardens extend to 120 acres.